VIVIENNE WESTWOOD

PROVOCATEUR

VIVIENNE WESTWOOD

PROVOCATEUR

Caroline Young

G:

I AM NOT A TERRORIST
please don't arrest me
I AM EXPEN SIV
PROPAGANDA
Organized Lying
Stop Distraction
Organized
EVERY DAY!

Ph. Jaime Navarro

MOS developed this masterplan where new prototypes for single-family houses and new models for urbanism came together in a *Laboratorio* (Laboratory). Thirty-two different offices participated with proposals to form a new community. PRODUCTORA was one of them (see p. 178) together with DVCH De Villar Chacón Arquitectos, Frida Escobedo, Dellekamp Arquitectos | Derek Dellekamp & Jachen Schleich, Rozana Montiel Estudio de Arquitectura, Ambrosi | Etchegaray, Zooburbia, Zago Architecture, Taller | Mauricio Rocha + Gabriela Carrillo, Taller de Arquitectura X, Griffin Enright Architects, Tatiana Bilbao Estudio, Francisco Pardo Arquitecto, Enrique Norten | TEN Arquitectos, Pita & Bloom, BGP Arquitectura, Zeller & Moye, Accidental Estudio de Arquitectura, Nuño - MacGregor - De Buen Arquitectos SC, SAYA+ Arquitectos, Cano | Vera Arquitectura, Fernanda Canales, RNThomsen Architecture, Agraz Arquitectos SC, Rojkind Arquitectos, Tactic-A, Gaeta-Springall Arquitectos, Taller ADG, Taller 4:00 A.M., CRO Studio, JC Arquitectura, and DCPP arquitectos.

Software No. 12
DROOP

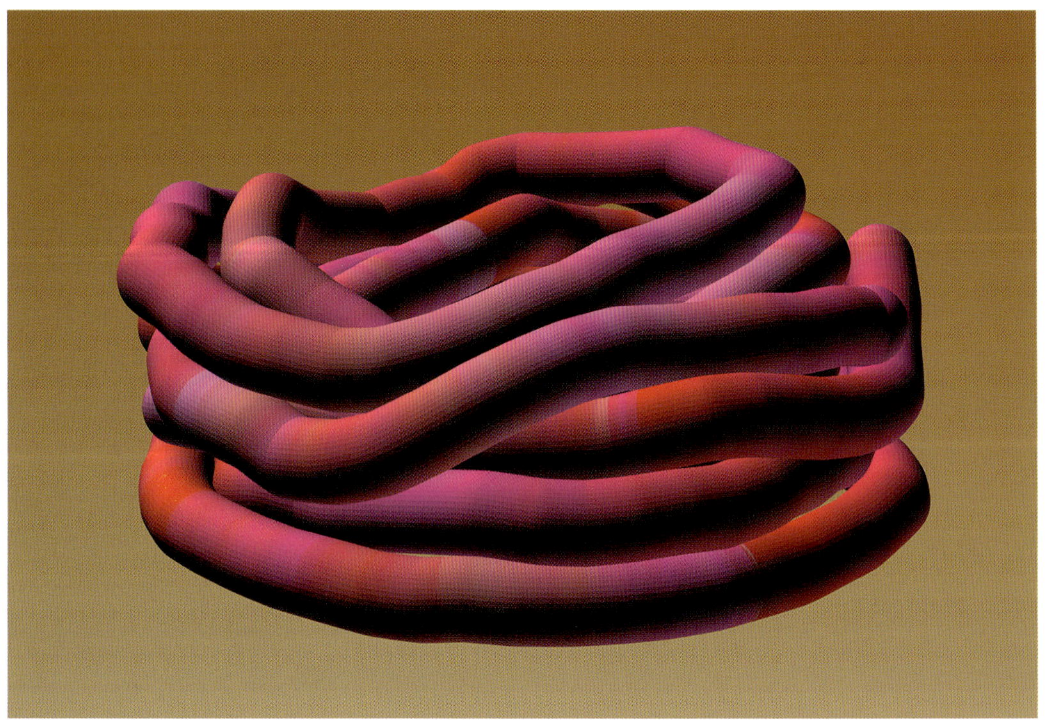

CONTENTS

INTRODUCTION

In September 2012, Vivienne Westwood made an unforgettable appearance at the closing ceremony of the London Paralympics. She had skipped the dress rehearsals so that she could retain an element of surprise, and as she took to the stage, outfitted as the warrior queen Boudica in a slogan T-shirt and tiny shorts, and with black lines on her face to represent a non-smiley face, she unfurled a huge banner printed with the words "Climate Revolution". It officially marked her new era – one where she would be a fervent eco-warrior, raising awareness through bold publicity campaigns for major environmental issues.

It was a fitting moment for the doyenne of fashion to steal the show at a major global event, as she had made a long career out of being a provocateur. From appearing as Margaret Thatcher on the cover of society magazine *Tatler* in 1989, to accidentally revealing she wasn't wearing knickers when she received her

"THERE WAS NO PUNK BEFORE ME AND MALCOLM ... AND THE OTHER THING YOU SHOULD KNOW ABOUT PUNK TOO: IT WAS A TOTAL BLAST."

LEFT Vivienne Westwood at her Seditionaries boutique in London, June 1977, during the height of the punk scene.

PAGE 2 Portrait of Vivienne, 2009.

PAGE 4 Presenting her Autumn/Winter collection, 2006.

ABOVE Vivienne at her studio in Battersea, London, 9 February 1996.

OBE from Queen Elizabeth II in 1992, she took every opportunity to shock, always with a wink at her off-beat humour. Vivienne was a contradiction in how she embraced and satirized royalty and tradition, from the "God Save the Queen" T-shirts and tartan bondage suits designed to sneer at the patriotism of the Golden Jubilee in 1977, to the orb in her logo and the heavy use of tartan and tweed as a bow to British tradition and craftmanship. She may have sent up images of the queen during her punk years, but she fully embraced her damehood when she received the honour in 2006.

Flamboyant, creative, politically conscious and fearless in delivering meaningful statements with outrageous acts, Vivienne Westwood didn't just create style; she was a style icon. It was Vivienne and her partner at the time, Malcolm McLaren, who were founders of the punk movement, and together with the Sex Pistols were the defining voice of disaffected youth in the 1970s. "There was no punk before me and Malcolm," she said. "And the other thing you should know about punk too: it was a total blast."

As the quintessential British designer, she was responsible for some of the most memorable fashion moments of all time – from Sid Vicious and Johnny Rotten in her obscene T-shirts to new wave artists in her foppish Pirate collection, to Naomi Campbell's tumble on the catwalk in sky-high platform heels, and Sarah Jessica Parker in the 2008 *Sex and the City* movie in her voluminous wedding dress.

"THE LAST THING I'M INTERESTED IN IS KEEPING UP WITH THE TIMES ... IF YOU KEEP UP WITH THE TIMES YOU'RE ALWAYS JUST MISSING SOMETHING."

ABOVE Vivenne during the late 1990s.

And like all true style revolutionaries, she was often misunderstood. In 1988, Vivienne was invited to appear as a guest on the primetime BBC television show *Wogan* with Sue Lawley, but as she showcased some of the pieces from her Time Machine collection, the audience sniggered and jeered. "Are people supposed to laugh?" Lawley baited. They failed to understand that what she was showcasing was not just pioneering and inventive, but exquisitely tailored. Vivienne was a committed researcher, delving deep into the history books and archives to discover new influences, and practising cutting techniques to construct her clothing with minimal waste. "In clothes, I work according to the cutting principle, not the draping principle," she said.[1]

She was born in Derbyshire during the Second World War, when Britain struggled under rationing due to a lack of resources, and her life's work would be about reusing, recycling, reinterpreting. In her memoirs, Vivienne noted that she could date everything that happened in her life to 1958, when she was 17 and her family moved from Derbyshire to London, so that her parents could run a post office in Harrow. She enrolled in and dropped out of art school, trained to be a teacher, got married and had a child. When she met Malcolm in the mid-1960s her expressive side came into its own, and she absorbed all that was happening with youth culture at the time. When her mother came to see one of Vivienne's later shows, she was amazed at how her daughter had managed to dream it all up. "I told her it wasn't dreaming, it was just hard work."[2]

Her early designs, including the Teddy boy suits and provocative T-shirts that she and Malcolm sold from their King's Road boutique, all had their origins in teenage self-expression and 1950s street style. She also experimented with her own image, shearing and bleaching her hair, dying it rainbow colours, wearing leather dominatrix gear and purple lipstick, obscenely funny slogan T-shirts, velvet leopard-print trousers – it was a mix of retro, DIY and bricolage, and a new way of presenting herself to the world.

ABOVE Walking the catwalk during the Vivienne Westwood Red Label Spring/Summer 2011 show at London Fashion Week, 19 September 2010.

By 1980, after punk fashion had become more ubiquitous on the runway, Vivienne was looking for a new direction and she settled on history. Pirate, in 1981, was her first collection to be shown on the catwalk and it was the one that finally made her feel like she was a fashion designer. It also marked the beginning of a deep fascination with the history of costume, and a desire to explore it through an intellectual lens. Inspired by eighteenth-century buccaneers and fops, with their pirate boots and poet-sleeved blouses, it attracted an adoring, and alternative, fanbase. Having broken from Malcolm McLaren in the mid-80s, and bravely decided, as a working mother with two boys, to go it alone, she faced many years of financial struggles. But by the 1990s she was a major attraction at Paris Fashion Week, and she could always be relied upon for a witty and outrageous catwalk moment. As her collections gained a loyal following in the '80s and '90s, she demonstrated her meticulous research into history and art, borrowing from the past to create something completely fresh and contemporary.

She played with the textures and colours in the works of eighteenth-century painters Jean-Antoine Watteau and François Boucher, and heightened the feminine silhouette with her modern interpretation of the crinoline skirt, the platform

shoes, the "Stature of Liberty" corset and the bum padding. At the same time, she claimed she didn't care for modern fashion. "The last thing I'm interested in is keeping up with the times," she said in 2004. "If you keep up with the times you're always just missing something."[3]

As she studied and subverted the techniques from past centuries, she led the way for other designers like John Galliano and Alexander McQueen to also reinterpret fashion history. She considered fashion a more exciting means of expression than art, because of the constraints of the human body in how the cloth would drape.[4]

By the 2000s, the woman who had presented the safety pin as an avant-garde fashion piece was attracting a loyal following of

ABOVE Vivienne in a giant bird cage to protest against the extradition of WikiLeaks founder Julian Assange to the USA, outside the Old Bailey court in London, July 2020.

celebrities like Helena Bonham Carter, Kate Winslet and Nigella Lawson, who appreciated her corsetry and boned underpinnings. "My fashion isn't for everybody," she said. "You have to have something very strong about your personality to want to wear my clothes."[5]

And then there was the politics. Vivienne declared her absolute interest in destroying conformity, and fashion was her tool to achieve it. With equal measures of provocation and flamboyance, Vivienne used her platform as a call to arms, and her political statements all had that punky, guerrilla, DIY feel which made her so exciting and energizing.

She always chose to defend the underdog, even if that was an unpopular choice. Some of the political causes she championed included fighting against fracking and industrial farming, protecting endangered species, supporting Scottish independence and fair working practices, and campaigning for the freedom of those she believed to be wrongly imprisoned, whether that was Leonard Peltier or WikiLeaks founder Julian Assange. From the 2010s, Vivienne's major focus was her climate revolution campaign, which she publicized as if it was an extension of the punk movement.

Vivienne was the visionary behind fetish-wear as fashion, bringing back the corset and reviving the Harris tweed industry, raising the platform of her shoes, using underwear as outerwear, inventing the tube skirt, and encouraging the safety pin to be worn in all sorts of places. Above all, her desire was to create ready-to-wear that looked like couture, and which was threaded with heroism. "They are larger than life, they help strike a figure, they have a sense of adventure about them," she insisted. "These clothes are strong and extreme. They don't hide you – they help you."[6]

She was one of the greatest talents of the twentieth century, who was still making an impact on fashion even into her eighties, and this is a celebration of a provocative life – from fashion and pop culture, to politics and environmentalism.

"YOU HAVE TO HAVE SOMETHING VERY STRONG ABOUT YOUR PERSONALITY TO WANT TO WEAR MY CLOTHES."

LTD
8
MAX REINHARDT
PUTNAM & COMPANY

1

THE MAKING OF A DESIGN REBEL

Born Vivienne Isabel Swire on 8 April 1941 in Glossop, Derbyshire, Vivienne had a simple and happy childhood which appeared, on the surface, to offer little clue as to how her life would turn out. "I lived in a part of the country that had grown up in the Industrial Revolution. I didn't know about art galleries until I was 17. I'd never seen an art book, never been to the theatre," she said. Yet it was a childhood shaped by love, storytelling and imagination, and what's more, as the daughter of shopkeepers, she had trade running in her blood.[7]

Her parents, Gordon Swire and Dora Ball, married just two weeks after the outbreak of the Second World War. Gordon had worked as a greengrocer, but with the first rumbles of war, he became a storekeeper in the Trafford Park munitions and aircraft factory. Here they made the Lancaster bombers that would blitz German cities and take part in the famous Dambusters Raid. Her mother, Dora, who had been a weaver in a cotton factory, was now also working for the war effort to make uniforms and parachutes when she was pregnant with her first child, Vivienne.

"I DIDN'T KNOW ABOUT ART GALLERIES UNTIL I WAS 17. I'D NEVER SEEN AN ART BOOK, NEVER BEEN TO THE THEATRE."

This construction of clothing was clearly in Vivienne's DNA. Her paternal grandfather, Ernest Swire, born in Glossop, was a bootmaker, and this skill, for making shoes, boots and clogs, had been passed down the generations throughout the nineteenth century.[8] Ernest and his brothers inherited the business from their father, and while they spent their days in the workshop, their sister Eleanor was a dressmaker. Gordon later converted the shop into a greengrocer's.

OPPOSITE Vivienne Westwood pictured in London, 30 August 1977.

"I STUDIED NATURE, READ, SEWED AND MADE THINGS CONSTANTLY."

"He was very entrepreneurial, good with his hands," said Vivienne of her father.[9] Dora's family was similarly involved in weaving and clog-making traditions; her father also worked as a cotton spinner, in a region of England that thrived in the Industrial Revolution to become a powerhouse of textile manufacturing.[10]

After Vivienne was born in 1941, she was followed by a sister, Olga, in 1944, and a brother, Gordon, in 1946. The family lived at 6 Millbrook, a two-storey house, one of a terrace of twelve workers' cottages in a hollow on the road between Hollingworth and Tintwistle, and it was surrounded by beautiful woodland and bluebell dells that were perfect for exploring. The cottage itself was constructed from thick stone walls, with stone window recesses, and a stone sink and pantry, and she enjoyed "'tippling' – doing handstands on the walls and flipping over the other side – and spent many happy hours playing marbles on the stone flags".[11]

The living room, warmed by the coal fire in the iron range, was the heart of the Swire home, and on cold evenings Dora entertained the family with songs and recitals of Romantic poetry and Grimm's fairy tales. "What we didn't have at home was any literature. I remember my mother once buying some encyclopedias but they weren't the right sort where you could look things up," she remembered.[12]

Born in the midst of wartime austerity, Vivienne's early life was shaped by rationing and scarcity. She didn't have a banana until she was seven, and her overwhelming memories were of endless knitting. Women would knit for their own families, to send to the front line, and for items that were unaffordable, such as wedding dresses when fabric was hard to come by. She remembered her mother having knitted her a brown dress with a little striped collar to wear to school, but at the time she didn't like it. What she really wanted was a princess dress in the style of the young princesses Elizabeth and Margaret.[13] She also remembered the parties served with jelly and blancmange and the cakes scattered with hundreds and thousands, the recycled clothing and improvised Christmas decorations that were her limited exposure to the war, and would forever symbolize the happiness of this beloved childhood.[14]

It was this "make do and mend" message, the "do-it-yourself" ethos cultivated in the war, that would shape the youth

ABOVE Vivienne in her studio in 2007. She developed her love of British textiles and DIY style from a childhood under rationing.

movements and subcultures of the next three decades, and would inspire Vivienne's early rocker, Teddy boy and punk collections. She had an awareness of the politics of fashion during this time, that "there was rationing and there were utility clothes – how many pockets you could have and no turn-ups – and you knew it, even as you pulled on your navy-blue utility knickers."[15] The utility clothes, and the local industry, would be evident in later designs, from the tweeds woven in the regional mills to the gabardine raincoats, and the way household objects such as the safety pin were stitched into the ethos of punk.

Vivienne's childhood instilled a love of the English countryside, and the traditions of riding, fishing and shooting, for which outdoor clothing is constructed from the fabrics woven in this textile heartland. This would also be a source of nourishment for her as a struggling mother trying to provide for her own children in the late '60s, when she had the knowledge to forage for her own food.

When Vivienne was a child, her mother would lift her over the back wall so she could play in the bluebells. The surrounding countryside was "beautiful and intimate until you reached the moors. Then it was wild and a little frightening. But I was perfectly happy alone, climbing trees and jumping streams."[16] She thought of herself as a tomboy at that time, but it had never occurred to her that she wanted to be a boy, or to have their freedoms. "I liked being me," she said, "and I happened to be a girl. I wanted to be a hero and saw no reason why a girl couldn't be one."[17]

She also showed an early tendency towards rebellion, and in an interview in 1992 for the BBC's *Desert Island Discs*, she recounted a story of how she was slapped by a teacher for going into the boys' toilet instead of the girls'. After having to queue up with the other girls during breaks, she didn't see why she couldn't use the other toilet instead. "And then I got branded as a sex maniac at the age of four," she added, with her customary dramatic flair for telling a story. "I'm quite innocent about a lot of things."[18]

She felt the need to attack injustice and to protect other children at school, and to defend those who were weaker; a quality that would be a lifelong trait when it came to her political causes. She was horrified when she first learned about the Crucifixion at her church school, which she said helped shape a desire to tackle injustice. "I felt I had to become a freedom fighter to stop this sort of thing going on. I really did want to do something to change this horrible world."[19]

"I WAS ADVENTUROUS, HIGH-SPIRITED AND CLEVER ... EVEN AT THE AGE OF FIVE, I COULD HAVE MADE A PAIR OF SHOES."

She was popular with the other pupils because, she said, "I was adventurous, high-spirited and clever."[20] She was also developing the skills to make clothes and shoes from a young age. "Even at the age of five, I could have made a pair of shoes," she said. Attending the local Tintwistle church school from the age of eight, she was given sewing classes where she learned to chain stitch, but what she most enjoyed was the lessons making dolls. She and her classmates would go to a teacher's house once a week to learn the process of constructing them. "These were the early clues to what I became – I studied nature, read, sewed and made things constantly."[21]

Another defining moment of her childhood was watching the coronation of Elizabeth II on 2 June 1953. Vivienne and her family

ABOVE Exhibits of Vivienne's early works, showing her "make do and mend" ethic, in the exhibition "35 Years in Fashion" at the Mori Arts Centre Gallery in Tokyo, Japan, 2007. In the foreground is the "kitchen sink" cardigan, made from dishcloth cotton and Vim scouring powder lid buttons.

attended a tea party at Tintwistle Sunday school, decked out with Union Jack bunting, and then gathered around the television in the living room of a neighbour's cottage to watch the live transmission from the BBC. This image of the beautiful young queen in her robes and jewels, with all the symbolism of royalty, tradition and ceremony, made a strong impression on Vivienne. While she and Malcolm McLaren mocked and satirized it with their punk emblem of the queen with a safety pin through her nose, she would also treat it seriously, with the adoption of the orb for her logo and the collections that were infused with an aristocratic edge.

When she was 11, her parents bought Tintwistle post office, having saved up the £100 to purchase it, and at that time she also passed the entrance exam for Glossop Grammar School. She loved studying English literature and history, and she was the type of student who raised her hand first. By the age of 14, she had also turned her attention to boys. Her mother, Dora, who was always well turned out, inspired a similar confidence in her children, ensuring they were well dressed with items purchased from C&A in Manchester, or by making their clothes herself.

Now, as a teenager, Vivienne padded her bras because she knew the boys liked the big breasts of stars like Marilyn Monroe and Jayne Mansfield, and wore homemade pencil skirts, a relatively new and provocative item, which imbued in her a sense of power, and which she described as "the most exciting garment ever designed".[22] Vivienne blossomed at the age of 14, as her "stick out teeth" were straightened, and as she experimented with make-up, high-heeled shoes and bras, her confidence that she was going to be "terribly pretty" was fully realized.

Shopping in Manchester one day, she was stopped in her tracks at the sight of a pair of stilettos in the window of a shoe shop. She had never seen something so sexual and provocative, and after buying a pair, she turned up at school wearing them with her pencil skirt, looking a "sensation".[23] She was continually experimenting with her style to be more eye-catching, and more unusual, than anyone else. Decades ahead of Geri in the Spice Girls, she dyed her long brown hair red and added a bleached stripe.

By the time she was in her mid-teens, the rock 'n' roll movement, imported from America, was infiltrating Britain and

ABOVE A group of teenage boys queue up at the hairdressers for their Teddy boy hair styles, England, 1953.

OPPOSITE Dancing to rock 'n' roll music at the Crown and Anchor pub in Brixton, south London, September 1956.

driving a new teenage rebellion, where music and fashion was an outlet for boredom and disaffection. Rationing was still in place in Britain up until 1954, and it was a desperate, austere time, driving young people to look towards the utopia of the United States instead. All-American anti-heroes like Marlon Brando, James Dean and Elvis Presley rebelled in their white T-shirts and jeans, traditionally the uniform of the working man. The Teddy boy subculture emerged around this time, as young working-class men fused together two opposing worlds. They emulated the upper-class Edwardian style of fashionable Mayfair gentlemen in their narrow suits and drainpipe trousers, and infused it with the swagger of a gunfighter in Hollywood westerns with their long draped jackets, thin bootlace ties, and "duck's arse" Brylcreemed hair. In 1954, Bill Haley's 'Shake, Rattle and Roll' became the first rock 'n' roll success in Britain, and the Teddy boys were now hooked on the mood and the sound, which was the perfect channel for youth, energy and rebellion, which soon sparked a moral panic in the media. "I was not a rebel, but it was a great age to be a teenager, because the look was all about rebellious youth versus age," she said. "This all, later on, appealed to Malcolm. I had a certain devilry about me, and in that sense I was very suited to rock 'n' roll."[24]

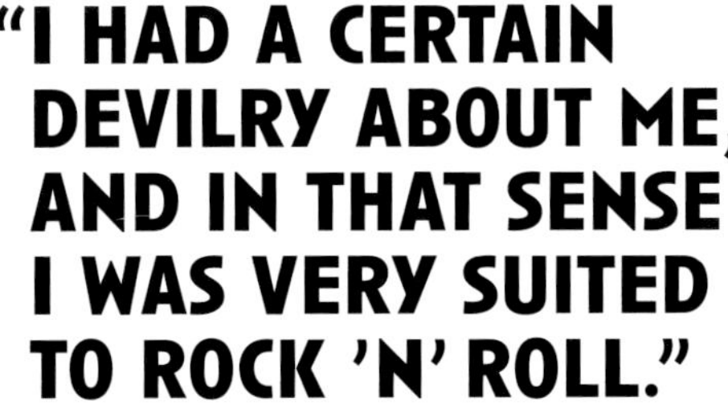
"I HAD A CERTAIN DEVILRY ABOUT ME, AND IN THAT SENSE I WAS VERY SUITED TO ROCK 'N' ROLL."

As studious as she was, Vivienne had no concept of what she would do once she left school, as women's opportunities tended to be limited to being a schoolteacher, a nurse or a secretary. Her life trajectory, however, would shift at the age of 17. Her parents realized they would have a better chance of thriving if they moved south, and so, in early 1958 they moved to Harrow, a town in Middlesex (now north-west London). They purchased the post office at 31 Station Road, which was also attached to the local general store, and set up home in the flat above. She credited this change with altering the course of her life.

Now that she had finished school, Vivienne applied for Harrow Art School, where she enrolled in a dressmaking course. She found that her fellow classmates were traditional jazz devotees who dressed in a particular style, known as "trad". Vivienne also became a follower, shifting from the pencil skirts to full skirts, sloppy knitted jumpers and a headscarf tied around her hair, and like the bohemian artist of her mind, she walked barefoot while carrying her art materials in a basket.

Disappointed that her course was more focused on drawing, when she was desperate to learn the practicalities of making clothes, she transferred to silversmithing, but after one term, dropped out of art college altogether. If she was going to be a dressmaker, she needed to earn money to develop her career, and so she took a Pitman's typing course to train to be a secretary, while working at the Kodak factory in Harrow. She soon realized that secretarial work wasn't for her, and instead studied for a Diploma of Education at St Gabriel's teacher training college in Camberwell, south London, where she specialized in art.

Vivienne hadn't found "any sexual vitality amongst the beards and the cider" of the alternative scene at art college, and instead was more attracted to the type of "bloke" found in the dance halls in the north of England who was more likely to approach her and ask her out. She began running with a new mod crowd who would go to pubs and dances together, to Ronnie Scott's for jazz or to the ballroom in nearby Queensbury. "That was my social life: cars and pubs and dancing," she said.[25]

These "original" mods were different in style to the later pop art mod fashions of the 1960s. This first incarnation were afficionados of American modern jazz, worshipping the style of Charlie Parker and Miles Davis, while casting an eye to Europe for the boxy Italian jackets known as "bumfreezers", the Brioni suits, the Vespa scooters so prevalent in Italy and the new espresso bars that were popping up in Soho and the West End. Vivienne began dressing like the mod girls, with her pencil skirts, winklepicker shoes and beehive hair.[26]

She was coming of age among a post-war generation of young people who were creating new cultures through fashion and music, and in a stagnated economy, were finding a new way to express themselves. Generous art college grants were taken up by those who would become the groundbreaking cultural figures of the era, like Mary Quant, John Lennon, and Pete Townshend from the Who. When Quant opened her Chelsea shop, Bazaar, in

OPPOSITE A female fashion model, wearing a black and white harlequin check coat and pattered tights, posing outside the Bazaar fashion boutique, September 1964. Owned by fashion designer Mary Quant, the shop was located at 138a King's Road in Chelsea, London.

1955, she launched the concept of the boutique, a hub for young people to try hip new clothes while listening to records. It was an exciting, vibrant time, and by 1960 the UK's economic recovery was bolstering success and driving up ambition.

In late 1961, at a dance, Vivienne met Derek Westwood, an apprentice at the Hoover factory in west London who had ambitions to be a pilot, which he later achieved. Derek was part of her circle of mods, as he was working as a club promoter to organize dances. "He was very lively and ever such a good dancer," she said.[27] She and Derek married on 21 July 1962 at a church in Greenhill, with Vivienne in a wedding dress that she had made herself, because by this time she was "very handy with a needle and thread" and had "a perfect figure".[28]

After their wedding, they moved into a red-brick terraced house at 86 Station Road, near her family's post office, and their son, Ben, was born a year later. Vivienne had been working as a teacher while assisting Derek with his club nights and gigs for the Rolling Stones and later for the Who, manning the cloakroom while pregnant, but she felt restless in her marriage. She needed more than a life of domesticity. While he tried to persuade her to stay, she left him in 1965, moving into her parents' flat with three-year-old Ben. With her creative spirit she had a deep desire to explore her intellectual and cultural life, and, she said, "I needed brain stimulation and I didn't know how to find it."[29]

ABOVE LEFT Vivienne in regal attire, 1992.

OPPOSITE Vivienne Westwood patent leather bag with orb logo, 2009.

GOD SAVE THE QUEEN
SHE AIN'T NO HUMAN BEING

2

THE ROCK SHOP

OPPOSITE Vivienne and Malcolm outside Bow Street Magistrate Court, 8 June 1977, after Malcolm was remanded on bail for fighting during their Jubilee boat trip.

After leaving her husband, Vivienne was now a single mother living above the family post office with her son Ben, while teaching art at Furness Primary School in north-west London. She supplemented her income by utilizing her art college training in silversmithing to make and sell jewellery at Portobello Road market.

Her younger brother, Gordon, enrolled at Harrow Technical College, would introduce her to a figure who would have a monumental impact on the creativity and intellectualism she sought. "The story of my life can largely be told via the men who are important to me," she reflected in 2004, and Malcolm Edwards (later McLaren) would be a major influence.[30]

Malcolm would be called "the most evil man in the world" by John Lydon, aka the Sex Pistols' Johnny Rotten, and "the pirate king of British pop" by *GQ* as he created new movements from the most unlikely of origins. As manager of the Sex Pistols, and later Bow Wow Wow, he became a favourite of 1970s tabloid journalism as a figure people loved to hate; a vicious Svengali and puppet-master who unleashed foul-mouthed vulgarians onto the British public.

Born in 1946, he described a neglected childhood of abandonment as a baby, before being taken in by his grandmother, an overbearing figure who slept in the same bed with him until he was 14. At 19, Malcolm was studying at Harrow Art School, which shared a canteen with the technical college, and he and Gordon bonded over their worship of '50s Teddy boy style. He was a striking-looking teenager with red hair and the palest skin that he further emphasized with talcum powder, and he was also sleeping rough in the cemetery at Harrow-on-the-Hill.

Gordon had taken pity on him, letting him use his car to bed down at night. Malcolm would often visit the Swires' flat with Gordon, and offered to help Vivienne with her jewellery-making. Impressed by his mod designs, she was immediately drawn to this "extraordinary creature from another planet; it was his ideas that attracted me to him."[31]

Vivienne, Malcolm and Gordon went to parties together where they would debate politics, and he would regale her with his ideas for art projects, or "installations", as he called them. They were living through a period of great change, where post-war gloom had made way for a burst of British creativity in fashion, music, art and film. At the same time there was a pressure of instability in the air with the ongoing Cold War and the fervent countercultural protests, and Malcolm's intellectualism tapped into both.

To Vivienne, Malcolm was "like a god, as he knew so many things – a pot of gold at the end of rainbow." She wouldn't do everything he wanted, which later included a plan to set fire to the Beatles waxworks at Madame Tussauds, because of her concerns that people could get hurt, but, she said, "I was very pleased to have that relationship and I learnt an awful lot from being with him."[32]

"[MALCOLM WAS AN] EXTRAORDINARY CREATURE FROM ANOTHER PLANET; IT WAS HIS IDEAS THAT ATTRACTED ME TO HIM."

When she met Malcolm, she was "into the dolly bird look. Wispy hair and fur coats", and as she was taught about politics and radical art, she became a canvas for his stylings. He spent part of his student grant furnishing her with school-girl dresses from John Lewis which were worn with white collars and ankle socks, and tight red rubberized cotton macs. After two years, their friendship crossed into a sexual one when Malcolm, sensing her mothering instinct, feigned being sick, and after spending all day as his carer, she climbed into bed next to him.

Their son, Joseph, was born on 30 November 1967, and they gave him the Portuguese surname Corré from Malcolm's grandmother. Malcolm, who romanticized the student protest movements against capitalism and war, was turned off by living with a single mother and schoolteacher. But she covered the rent for an apartment in Aigburth Mansions, near the Oval in

Kennington, and took care of all the childcare, cooking and cleaning while he continued to study art. He would stay in bed in the mornings rather than take Joe to nursery, which meant she would regularly be late for work as a supply teacher at a school in Brixton; a tiring job that required a bundle of energy to teach the 80 kids in her class.[33] The years she spent working as a teacher while raising her children were very hard. With the evenings taken up with cooking and cleaning, while also balancing the class preparation for the next day, she was perpetually exhausted.[34]

Malcolm was focused on his installations inspired by the French situationists; *agents provocateurs* who took part in "happenings" to push bold statements as a reaction to the status quo. On one occasion he and Jamie Reid, later the creator of punk iconography like the "God Save the Queen" artwork, barricaded themselves into Croydon College's art school to make a series of ridiculous demands, such as being able to sculpt in pure gold. Another stunt took place at Selfridges department store, where he and a group of fellow students gave away toys as a protest against consumerism.[35]

In May 1968, student protests broke out around the Latin Quarter of Paris, and their slogans, "Be reasonable: Demand the impossible" and "Under the paving stones lies the beach", would later be adopted by Malcolm and Vivienne as manifestos printed on their T-shirts. In this way situationism played an important role in shaping punk as a provocative movement driven by bold fashion statements that were impossible to ignore.

When the pressures of her life became too much to cope with, Vivienne quit her job, and without the salary to pay the rent, she walked out on Malcolm, and took the children to her parents' caravan in North Wales. She survived on a government family allowance, and with her knowledge of edible plants she foraged for food, such as using dandelions to make salads.[36] Malcolm persuaded her to come back to London, and in spring 1969 they moved into 10 Thurleigh Court, Nightingale Lane, in Clapham, and she took up another teaching job to support the family.[37]

The next decade would be marked by a rise in unemployment, union action and strikes. From the sexual revolution of the 1960s, Britain was also slowly becoming a more permissive society. Homosexuality was decriminalized in 1967, and that same year abortions were also legalized. Combined with the increased availability of the contraceptive pill and the gains of the feminist movement, women were able to explore their freedoms more than ever before. Late '60s youth culture had been dominated by the hippie movement, and so, by 1970, a Teddy boy revival was rising up as a working-class reaction against the middle-class students who preached peace and love.

The King's Road was becoming the epicentre of alternative style, and the number one rock 'n' roll purveyor was Mr Freedom, owned by Tommy Roberts and Trevor Myles, and which opened at number 430 in 1969. The name came from the spoof anti-war movie from 1969, and the boutique similarly skewered hippies by catering to a new glam rock mood. Its velvet and leopard print, satin jackets and thunderbolt motifs were snapped up by stars like Elton John and Rod Stewart. Vivienne was awed by the clothing in Mr Freedom and joyfully purchased a pair of tight leopard-print velvet trousers. "I had never seen anything like it. It was the most amazing thing," she remembered.[38]

As well as shopping in the boutiques on the King's Road, she would also create her own curiosities. She teamed circle and pencil skirts in bright fabrics with snakeskin heels and bobbysocks; a peacocking that was guaranteed to soak up

BELOW The Sex Pistols were regular visitors to the King's Road shop, and were greatly influenced by its fashion. Showing (l to r) Johnny Rotten, Paul Cook, Sid Vicious and Steve Jones, 1976.

"I'VE ALWAYS BEEN A REBEL. I STOPPED TRAFFIC SOMETIMES."

ABOVE A rare pair of knickers designed by Vivienne Westwood and Malcolm McLaren in the 1970s.

attention. "I've always been a rebel. I stopped traffic sometimes," she said. "I remember one time I was on the zebra crossing in front of the shop on King's Road, in a rubber negligee with my hair all in spikes, and a man said to me ... 'Does your bush look like that?'"[39]

Malcolm had persuaded her to cut off her long brown hair, and the swinging London hairstylist Leonard of Mayfair sheared it into a crop. She then customized it further by bleaching it and using a razor to create a spiky, shaggy 'do.[40] Gene Krell, co-owner of the Granny Takes a Trip boutique at 488 King's Road, remembered his first "unforgettable" sighting of Vivienne in "tight, velvet leopardskin-print slacks and black patent booties with a stiletto heel, she had spiky blonde hair. I was staggered by her style, and had to find out more, to understand it."[41]

Vivienne's personal life was a struggle, but through her unique style, the bleach blonde crop that was ahead of David Bowie's Ziggy Stardust and his punky spiked and dyed hair, and the

"TEDDY BOYS ARE FOREVER – ROCK IS OUR BUSINESS."

Let It Rock ethos

clothing that she picked up from the King's Road boutiques, she found a strength and power in feeling like "a space princess" in velvet leopard-print trousers, troubadour shirts printed with hearts and spades, a glittering lurex headscarf from Woolworths, and purple lipstick.[42]

After he finally graduated in summer 1971, Malcolm fell into a depression as to what he would do with his life. He used his passion for rock 'n' roll as a business opportunity, where he could sell records and nostalgic fanzines and magazines, and the vintage Bakelite radios that he restored to working order. He and Vivienne went down to Brick Lane every Saturday to buy rock 'n' roll records and second-hand clothing, which they initially sold at a market stall. When a new South Pacific-themed boutique, Paradise Garage, took over from Mr Freedom at 430 King's Road, they were invited to share the space. Malcolm was quick to take advantage of the opportunity and in November 1971 they claimed the entire shop. They installed fluorescent pink letters above the door to spell out the name, Let It Rock, alongside their ethos: "Teddy boys are Forever – Rock is our business."

Vivienne gave up teaching and purchased a Singer sewing machine to help her restore original Teddy boy drape coats, with Malcolm picking out the most authentic buttons to replace the missing ones. When they sold out of the original pieces, Vivienne began making copies, unpicking the suits to work out how to duplicate them, and commissioning tailor Sid Green to create neon drape jackets which she then customized with velvet or sequined collars.[43] Because it was a revival of a subculture that was less than 20 years old, there was plenty of original stock to be sourced, including winkle-pickers, drainpipe trousers, and brothel creepers – although, in this Teddy boy revival, dripping with glam rock influence, the soles were now stacked much higher. She also sold her own designs, knitting beatnik-style mohair jumpers, worn oversized and with tights, as if borrowing a boyfriend's, and bright, button-up satin dresses that clung to the body.

The shop was a Mecca for the teenagers who worshipped the rebelliousness of rock 'n' roll, and its floor was styled like a mid-century living room. Its walls were plastered with images of James Dean, Elvis and bombshell pin-ups, while a jukebox blasted out Gene Vincent and Eddie Cochran, and cabinets

OPPOSITE Teddy Boy Malcolm McLaren outside his newly opened shop on the King's Road, Chelsea, with assistant Addie Chase, March 1972.

LET IT
ROCK

displayed Brylcreem, plastic combs and sweetheart lockets. In a May 1972 feature in *The Sunday Times Magazine*, Let It Rock was described as the only shop selling the "real thing" and "like walking into a flashback from the Fifties". The article estimated that with around twenty thousand revivalist Teddy boys in England, "the drainpipe-trouser trade is booming."

In the accompanying fashion spread, rock band Screaming Lord Sutch, in their Teddy boy suits, posed next to models dressed in Vivienne's satin dresses, worn unbuttoned to the crotch and paired with suede heels. Teds could also buy off-the-peg drape suits, which were made from the fabrics Malcolm personally sourced "to give them an authentic touch".[44]

In June 1972, Let It Rock was also namechecked in the *Evening Standard* as the place for "Greasers" to hang out. "There are vast

LEFT A sign outside the Let It Rock shop, advertising its wares for Teddy Boys and their girls, 1972.

numbers of Greasers all over the country between the ages of 14 and 25 united by their passion for the motorcycle; it gives them their name, their *raison d'etre*," the article said. "Mr Malcolm McLaren of the shop Let It Rock in the King's Road tells me that Greasers can pay up to £50 – £60 for a suit, a drape jacket in the Teddy Boy style with velvet collar, and drainpipe trousers. They wear it with fluorescent socks and creepers (thick crepe soled shoes), in blue, black, red, yellow or purple."[45]

The press coverage for Let It Rock focused on Malcolm, with no mention of Vivienne, even though she was in the back rooms working her sewing machine to create the drape suits, satin dresses and mohair jumpers. Malcolm would also downplay her efforts, telling *GQ* in 2000 that she was "never a creative thinker, never an innovator". When she was asked for her reaction, she replied: "It's a terrible shame Malcolm is still making the same comments after all these years."

He considered himself the British Andy Warhol, whereas she was one of the puppets he manipulated for his creative installations. Yet it was Vivienne's style, her foresight, that made the shop so unique. Without her designs, the reinvigoration of the Teddy boy suits, the satin dresses, he wouldn't have earned the coverage of these early days.

On 5 August 1972, a major rock 'n' roll concert, The London Rock and Roll Show, was held at Wembley Stadium with performances by Chuck Berry, Little Richard and Bill Haley & His Comets. To cater to the new Teddy boys, Vivienne and Malcolm customized T-shirts to sell at the event, but these failed to shift, and she used the surplus stock to experiment with new designs. She converted the cotton tees into knickers branded with "Let It Rock" lettering, studs and images of Little Richard and 1950s pin-up girls. The T-shirts were also customized with '50s turn-up sleeves, printed with pin-up girls, and situationist slogans, including "Under the paving stones lies the beach." It was a retro and kitsch do-it-yourself aesthetic with a radical message, and these new slogan T-shirts became more popular than the zoot suits and brothel creepers.

After the pink letters of Let It Rock began to fall apart, Vivienne and Malcolm rebranded the shop as "Too Fast to Live Too Young to Die". With its clear reference to James Dean, it would now focus on the motorbike-riding rockers and "greasers". The drape

RIGHT Dancing at The London Rock and Roll Show held in Wembley Stadium, London, 5 August 1972.

LONDON ROCK

"I HAD MY SAMPLE MACHINIST, ANNE, IN THE LIVING ROOM AND LOCAL ROCKERS DECORATING OUR CLOTHES WITH CHAINS, BADGES AND STUDS."

jackets were replaced with bikers' jackets, chains, Levi's and rocker memorabilia. "There was a chapter of Hells Angels down the road," Vivienne said. "I had my sample machinist, Anne, in the living room and local rockers decorating our clothes with chains, badges and studs."[46]

The slogan tees became a major part of their stock because they appealed to young people as a means of displaying their beliefs, and their contempt for society, on their chests. She created these T-shirts at the kitchen table in her home, hand-stencilling and potato printing, gluing, sewing and cutting. Black sleeveless T-shirts were customized with studs to spell out VENUS and SCUM, the name of the radical feminist group founded by Valerie Solanas, notorious for her attempted murder of Andy Warhol in 1968. ROCK was formed with chain-linked bleached chicken bones, and other popular designs featured zip details over the nipple area.[47] Vivienne repurposed everyday items that would likely be thrown out otherwise, and not only was she harking back to the rationing of the war, but she was prefiguring the later trends for recycling and upcycling. They were also radical in their incorporation of graphic art, known as "Lettrism", and would be an early incarnation of the slogan T-shirts that made Katharine Hamnett's name.

The shop was becoming a hip draw for edgy rock 'n' roll stars including Iggy Pop, Marianne Faithfull, Jimmy Page and the Kinks, but it was also a gathering place for disaffected teenagers. Now in her thirties, Vivienne was older than the greasers and Teddy boys who were drawn to the shop, and while she was often motherly to them, she was also the most original in her self-expression. Her son Ben remembered her, in 1973, wearing "really short skirts and having blonde spiky hair. I remember going round to see boarding schools and the other kids were looking up her skirt and I was embarrassed."[48]

Their radical, but retro, designs earned Vivienne and Malcolm a commission, to create costumes for Ringo Starr and David Essex in the film *That'll Be the Day* (1973). It was a coming-of-age drama set in the late 1950s, in which Essex played a hedonistic teen who falls in with unruly rockers.

At the same time as Vivienne and Malcolm were lighting the first sparks of London's punk movement, there was also an underground punk scene brewing in New York City. They

OPPOSITE Showcasing the latest fashions from the King's Road in 1973 – including Let it Rock greaser wear and a pillbox hat from Mr Freedom.

ABOVE English pop star David Essex (l) with musician Ringo Starr on the set of the film *That'll Be The Day*, UK, in 1972. They both play barmen at a holiday camp.

were invited there in August 1973, alongside other King's Road boutiques, to showcase their wares at the National Boutique Show at the Hotel McAlpin. From their hotel room they set out all their T-shirts, Teddy boy suits and memorabilia, with Jerry Lee Lewis and Bill Haley blasting from a portable record player, but they sold nothing on that first day. The New York Dolls had visited the shop when in London, and the band's guitarist Sylvain Sylvain called into their hotel room to browse the makeshift stall. He not only convinced them that they should be staying at the Chelsea Hotel, the hedonistic, bohemian centre of underground culture, but he also invited them out to explore the East village punk clubs. They were featured in Andy Warhol's *Interview* magazine, saw performances of Richard Hell and Patti Smith at CBGB, and hung with Warhol's Factory gang.

When Too Fast to Live Too Young to Die went through another rebranding in 1974, this one would be even more controversial, and would be based on Malcolm's observation that "England is the home of the flasher, we're all closet pervs."[49] Now named SEX, it would cause such outrage that Vivienne would be arrested for obscenity; something that made her incredibly proud. It was an endorsement of the entire ethos of her designs, that the reason she was in fashion was to "destroy the word 'conformity'".

OPPOSITE Pamela Rooke aka Jordan, the Queen of punk rockers, at the new SEX shop on the King's Road, December 1976.

SEX

TELEPHONE
TELEPHONE
I've changed to
No.6

3

PUNK DISRUPTORS

OPPOSITE Vivienne Westwood (r) dressed in plaid, with Jordan (l) and a friend in London, 12 April 1977.

By the end of summer 1974, rubbery pink PVC lettering was now spelling out SEX over the entrance to 430 King's Road, as Vivienne and Malcolm fully embraced hardcore sexuality for their next incarnation. In a British society that leaned towards sexual repression, their aim, with their blatant, out-there fetishism, was to shock.

Unclothed, headless mannequins were piled together in the windows, and inside, gym exercise bars were a prop to display the whips and chains, nipple clamps and handcuffs, while a grubby double bed covered in a rubber sheet acted as a centrepiece.[50] The shop began to attract a range of customers, from the dominatrixes looking for the tools of their trade, to the city bankers with hidden kinks, who came to be fitted for one of Vivienne's rubber bodysuits, ordered from mail-order sex catalogues. "It was our first innovation ... I was walking around in rubber negligees and pointed-toe, high-heel shoes. Nowadays, you see people looking like this, but in those days, you only saw prostitutes looking that way," she told *Women's Wear Daily* in 1992.[51]

She insisted to the *Guardian* in 1977 that all her offerings were designed to be confrontational. "That was why I began making sexual clothing from materials such as leather and rubber, they make people far more willing to flaunt themselves and produce reactions."[52]

The slogan tees continued to be a major draw for the shop. One of the first under the SEX label was a deliberate provocation with the aim to be labelled "obscene". It was printed with the image of two cowboys facing each other, naked from the waist down, and with their penises nearly touching. The image proved to be particularly shocking due to a moral panic at the time sparked by the BBC documentary *Johnny Go Home*, featuring a teenage runaway who was forced to work as a rent boy.

"THEY KEPT ASKING ME WHERE I GET MY CLOTHES. THE POLICE SAID THAT THE TEE-SHIRT WASN'T THE KIND OF THING I SHOULD BE WEARING IN THE AREA OF PICCADILLY CIRCUS."

Alan Jones, the *Guardian*

In August 1975, Alan Jones, a 24-year-old hotel receptionist at the funky Portobello Hotel, was walking through Piccadilly Circus wearing the naked cowboy T-shirt when he was stopped by two plain-clothed policemen. After much questioning about the T-shirt, he was taken down to the station and charged with an offence under the 1824 Vagrancy Act. "They kept asking me where I get my clothes. The police said that the tee-shirt wasn't the kind of thing I should be wearing in the area of Piccadilly Circus," he told a reporter.[53] SEX was then raided by the police, 18 offensive T-shirts were seized, and Vivienne and Malcolm were also charged with "exposing to public view an indecent exhibition". It was a proud moment for them, and after being fined £50, they started to sell their most offensive T-shirts under the counter.

One of their most popular T-shirts was "Tits", from 1976, which was printed with a pair of naked breasts, and which was selected by Alice Cooper when he visited the shop. Another was printed with a list of likes and dislikes, which formed a manifesto titled "You're gonna wake up one morning and know what side of the bed you've been lying on!" As an early version of the "what's hot and what's not" features that became a staple of magazines, their list of "Hates" included Mick Jagger, *Vogue* magazine and the Metropolitan Police, while their "Loves" included Joe Orton, Eddie Cochran, Christine Keeler, militant feminist group SCUM, and Kutie Jones and his Sex Pistols – the early band founded by Pistols' guitarist Steve Jones.[54]

Malcolm insisted they were his concepts, and that Vivienne "did not have any ideas. She did not think of herself as being creative, but she was phenomenally good with her hands. She was a great little researcher. She would find a way to make an idea work."[55] Vivienne, however, was adamant that the T-shirts were vital to her concerns with delivering a message of intent against the establishment. "Malcolm's motives weren't political like mine, but he had this great idea of using sex to confront and shock," she said in 2004. "To him England was the country

ABOVE The Tits dress, 1974, as featured in the later exhibition celebrating Westwood's work at the Victoria and Albert Museum, London, 2004.

ABOVE RIGHT The Cowboys handscreen printed T-shirt, 1976.

of sexually repressed closet cases and flashers. Hence the Sex Pistols, and all those T-shirts printed with DESTROY and ANARCHY. It was an exercise in the young throwing over the values of the old."[56]

Just as her fascination with the historical construction of clothing would drive her later work, she was interested in deconstructing the T-shirt in order to fully explore how its beauty lay in its simplicity. By breaking it down to its most basic components, she stitched two squares of cotton jersey along the shoulders and down the side, which created a tight, figure-hugging effect.[57]

The attraction for teenagers to SEX and its T-shirts was the shock factor, where they deliberately chose pieces that would disgust their parents and the older generation. These young, disenfranchised people were drawn to Malcolm and Vivienne's idolization of the criminals and anti-heroes – the Great Train Robbers, the highwayman Dick Turpin, Fagin from *Oliver Twist*

BE
REASONABLE
DEMAND
THE
INPOSSIBLE

became obsessed with the idea of creating a new rock band as an anarchic, situationist statement. Since he was a boy, Malcolm had been drawn to the idea of having a gang around him, realized in the art students that he would encourage to take part in stunts, and the disparate kids who gathered at his shops. From this unlikely group of rebellious, dangerous urchins, he formed his band, which would be clothed in the fashions from the shop, but with costs taken out of their royalties.

Steve Jones, along with his school friend Paul Cook, had been a regular since the days of Let It Rock, while Glen Matlock worked as a shop assistant there. John Lydon first made an appearance at the shop in August 1975, where he was nicknamed "Johnny Rotten" due to the state of his teeth. Simon John Ritchie, known as Sid Vicious, who was nihilistic, troubled and living in squats after being kicked out of home by his heroin addict mother, had been Vivienne's original suggestion for singer, but when he went AWOL, Johnny Rotten was chosen instead. He had first come into the shop one Saturday with his hair dyed green, and Malcolm immediately saw his potential as a frontman. "Johnny was very unpleasant," Vivienne recalled, "and the band never liked each other, but somehow it came together. We were all into this idea of anarchy. We hated the older generation, thought they'd mismanaged the world and turned it into a corrupt place. This is what the Sex Pistols were all about: Fuck the establishment – we don't accept your values and taboos."[60]

The Sex Pistols played their first gig on 6 November 1975 at Saint Martin's School of Art, with their crowd of provocative supporters dressed like the band on stage as they pogo danced in the crowded hall. Caroline Coon of the *Melody Maker* had coined the nickname the Bromley Contingent for this group of young, dedicated punks who bought (or stole) Vivienne's outrageous designs, or constructed their own to wear to clubs.

By the summer of 1976 there was a definite punk aesthetic, despite the individualistic DIY aspect to it: people now used everyday objects to uglify themselves to look as hostile and aggressive as possible. There were the safety pins through the ears and cheeks, dog leashes and bike locks around the necks, used tampons and loo chains dangling from jackets, clothes made from black bin bags, kettles as handbags, and ripped fishnet tights with stiletto heels.

There was also a punk tendency to take one of the most extreme, offensive symbols, the swastika, as a way of further provoking the establishment. Vivienne had been uneasy about it; she wanted her designs to trigger change, but it was the type of shocking statement Malcolm liked to make. Punks, they later insisted, weren't in league with the far right, it was just a way of being hated. "Malcolm, being Jewish, had his reasons for wanting to do that kind of thing," she said. "We weren't only rejecting the values of the older generation, we were rejecting their taboos as well."[61]

In May 1977, the punk movement was featured in the *Washington Post* as the first British youth movement since the mods and rockers, where bored teens were creating their own style as a reaction against the dreariness of everyday life. "Their get-up screams 'look at me' and if it takes shock or disgust or even Nazi insignia to get that attention, they are game to try it. Nothing is lost," the article said.[62] "It's all part of the shock," Vivienne told the paper. "The kids are breaking every myth that was ever handed to them. Swastikas are not meant as a symbol of fascism though some are taking it in the true sense and mothers and fathers are shocked."[63]

ABOVE Sid Vicious and Vivienne at the Sex Pistols gig at Notre Dame Hall, London on 15 November 1976.

OPPOSITE The Sex Pistols perform their last concert in Winterland, San Francisco, USA, 14 January 1978.

Vivienne's target was the cruelty and corruption of the world, and with her desire to quash the status quo, she began sewing the anarchy sign "A" as a label on her clothing.[64] She didn't see herself as a fashion designer at this time, more as a researcher who was helping Malcolm on his projects; a provocateur who was delivering a statement of intent. Johnny Rotten wrote in his autobiography that punk "had a lot to do with Vivienne Westwood. Malcolm took a lot of the praise, but I think she did most of the designs."

It was a conflation of different movements that were happening at the time. There was the irony of glam rock and the gender ambiguity of David Bowie, and the symbolism of Third Reich Germany, which was being played with as a statement in films including *The Night Porter* (1974) and Ken Russell's *Mahler* (1974) for which he had asked Vivienne and Malcolm to design sado-masochistic, Nazi-inspired costumes. With the Fagin and Oliver Twist aspect to Malcolm and the Sex Pistols, punk was further a condemnation of the economic decline of Britain, and of the poverty and desperation that was affecting its young

LEFT Pamela Rooke aka Jordan, and Simon Barker aka Six, modelling bondage gear from the Seditionaries boutique in 1977.

BELOW Vivienne wearing a felt Inside Out Jacket at Seditionaries in 1977, with shop assistant Michael Collins, wearing a Cambridge Rapist T-shirt produced by Malcolm McLaren a couple of years earlier.

ABOVE By 1976, the shop had become Seditionaries (shown here in 1977), complete with frosted windows concealing its interior from outside scrutiny and a tiny brass plaque by the door defiantly declaring "Clothes for Heroes".

people. Malcolm also elevated it to the philosophical realm with the slogans inspired by Spanish anarchist Buenaventura Durruti, the situationists and Karl Marx,[65] although, for the kids involved, their major concern was the shock value of dressing up. As Boy George later said, "It became political and all the things it was never meant to be. It was popular to pontificate about anarchy or socialism. All it was about in the beginning was dressing up and looking ridiculous and having fun."[66]

In December 1976, the shop underwent another shift, from SEX to Seditionaries, which was a reflection of Vivienne's call for sedition and anarchy. The pink letters were taken down, the shop hoarding was covered in protest graffiti, and the interior was dominated by a backdrop of a bombed-out Dresden, to play with the imagery of war.[67]

"WE WEREN'T ONLY REJECTING THE VALUES OF THE OLDER GENERATION, WE WERE REJECTING THEIR TABOOS AS WELL."

Now sold under the label "Clothes for Heroes", and the anarchist "A", the clothes carried a tag that declared they were "For soldiers, prostitutes, dykes and punks". As part of this punk uniform, Vivienne created bondage suits from black sateen, with the trousers split by zips down the legs and under the crotch, and with a parachute shirt that featured straps fixed with D-rings. As mimicry of both straitjackets and military kit with their parachute straps, they were designed to be an anti-fashion assault on consumerism. With the whole outfit costing £80 (the equivalent of around £500 today), it was far beyond the realm of affordability for most people. But Vivienne chose to create quality products from leather, top grade wool and mohair, all of which were costly.

"There was no way I could have made a sophisticated, elaborate range without it costing a lot," she told the *Guardian* in September 1977. "I wanted to use good material and the designing took a year so I am giving value for money. I don't mind if the kids just look and then interpret it in their own way. I know that a lot of punks care very much about having new clothes; that is what they want to spend money on. Is it any worse than spending it on discos and records?"[68]

If the bondage suits were too expensive for many of her customers, the T-shirts were a means of buying into the ethos. At Seditionaries, the slogan T-shirts continued to deliver messages of intent, juxtaposing pornography with the supposed innocence of American icons Mickey Mouse and Marilyn Monroe. Malcolm, like Andy Warhol, chose to subvert the symbols of American popular culture and consumerism, and Disney was a particular target for its supposed co-opting of childhood. Vivienne made a one-off T-shirt of an erect penis, with the semen dripping over an image of Marilyn Monroe, and the flaccid penis on the other sleeve, and another T-shirt depicting Mickey and Minnie Mouse having sex.

BELOW LEFT Soo Catwoman on the front cover of the first issue of *Anarchy In the U.K.*, a magazine designed by Vivienne, Jamie Reid and Sophie Richmond.

BELOW The Anarchy in the U.K. torn T-shirt, 1976.

OPPOSITE Vivienne modelling the tartan version of her bondage suit, 1977.

PULL

GOD Save THE QUEEN

OPPOSITE Joan Jett arrives at the Rock Music Awards show in Los Angeles, wearing a Sex Pistols T-shirt, leather jacket and blue jeans with studded belt, *c.* 1977.

While the bondage trousers were made by a Greek tailor, Mr Mintos, Vivienne created all her designs from her front room, working them up on her Singer sewing machine and screen printer. She was a mother raising two children, but at the same time she was completely focused on shaping this movement. Vivienne was beginning to receive her own press, and was profiled in the *Guardian* in September 1977. The article described her walking around Chelsea in a tartan bondage suit, with bleached, spiky hair, smeared pink make-up and little silver penises dangling from her earlobes. She was such an eccentric vision that she almost caused a Jaguar and a lorry to crash into one another, a young man tittered to his friends about her get-up, and two staid ladies muttered about how revolting it was. As Vivienne was quoted as saying in the article: "If you wear something really provocative or outrageous and make people sit up and take notice of you then you are taking a step towards being liberated."

The Sex Pistols were signed to a record deal in October 1976, and their first single, 'Anarchy in the U.K.', was released on 26 November 1976. For the cover art, Jamie Reid placed the Union Jack as a backdrop, pinned it with a safety pin and branded it with cut-out lettering on top, as if ripped from a newspaper headline. Vivienne then used this design to make T-shirts.

If Malcolm's plan was for his band to become hate figures by manipulating the media, then he achieved that goal with one of their first television interviews, in December 1976 on ITV.

"I KNOW THAT A LOT OF PUNKS CARE VERY MUCH ABOUT HAVING NEW CLOTHES; THAT IS WHAT THEY WANT TO SPEND MONEY ON. IS IT ANY WORSE THAN SPENDING IT ON DISCOS AND RECORDS?"

ABOVE Malcolm McLaren at the opening reception of his exhibition, "Impresario: Malcolm McLaren and the British New Wave", New Museum of Contemporary Art, New York, 14 September 1988. The show featured an installation of Sex Pistols ephemera, including T-shirts he designed with Vivienne.

Interviewer Bill Grundy provoked them into swearing, and the next day the newspapers were bursting with outrage. "The Filth and the Fury" blasted the headline in the *Daily Mirror*, and the newspaper declared them "punk rock 'nasties'" who were "boorish, ill-mannered, foul-mouthed, dirty, obnoxious and arrogant".

The moment catapulted the punk movement to the front pages and into homes across the nation, and they became, as the new moral panic, the latest hate figures. They were the encapsulation of the decade's disaffection, of the industrial strikes, and the inflation, now wrapped up in leather-clad, safety-pinned and ripped youthful aggression.

With the Sex Pistols wearing clothes from Seditionaries for the ITV interview (including Steve Jones in the naked breasts T-shirt), it proved to be the perfect advertising for punk, not only bolstering "Anarchy in the U.K." but also promoting the shop. "These kids represent the most original, exciting and alive movement we have had in a long time," Vivienne said in 1977. "The press has got it all wrong. The point about punks is that they change their ideas and behaviour all the time. The one conviction they all share is that they want something other than the dull, safe trapped life-style they see around them."[69]

The summer of 1977 was to be a joyous, patriotic celebration of Queen Elizabeth II's 25 years on the throne, but the Sex Pistols transformed it into a controversial "Summer of Hate" with the release of their punchy single 'God Save the Queen'. With international eyes focused on London, another overriding image of the Jubilee was Jamie Reid's desecration of the Cecil Beaton portrait of the queen, putting a safety pin through her nose.

The Sex Pistols' first label, EMI, had dropped them on the back of the Grundy interview, and though A&M Records then signed a new contract with them outside Buckingham Palace, it reacted to their behaviour by then cancelling them too. Finally, maverick record executive Richard Branson of Virgin Records was willing to take the risk. He invited Vivienne, Malcolm, the Sex Pistols and two hundred punks to a party on a Thames riverboat called the *Queen Elizabeth*, but when a fight broke out the police were called. Malcolm and Vivienne were arrested, spending the night at Bow Street Police Station until they were bailed by Branson. Tensions ran high against the leaders of this supposedly unpatriotic movement, and with Chelsea football club fans reacting with fury against the shop, the windows were boarded up to protect it from being destroyed.

A young groupie, Nancy Spungen, had arrived in London from New York in 1976 to seek out the Sex Pistols, and her volatile, heroin-fuelled relationship with Sid Vicious would end in tragedy. The punk movement became more political, more destructive, more anarchist, and Nancy's murder and Sid's death by overdose in 1979 was the symbol of this descent. For those who had founded it, the punk movement was over. It was still visible in society, with acid green mohawks and leather jackets on every high street, but for Vivienne, she was on to new things. "I realised there was no subversion without ideas. It's not enough to want to destroy everything," she said.[70]

Vivienne wanted to shift her focus to fashion, but when she arranged to meet Grace Coddington at British *Vogue* to show her the designs, Grace dismissed her as irrelevant. She would later wryly comment that the editor was wearing a mohair jumper, exactly like the ones she made and sold from her shop. In April 1977, Zandra Rhodes had brought punk into acceptable fashion when she used rips, safety pins and sink chains on the catwalk as part of her Conceptual Chic Collection, yet Vivienne continued to be treated as an outsider.

"THE ONE CONVICTION [PUNKS] ALL SHARE IS THAT THEY WANT SOMETHING OTHER THAN THE DULL, SAFE TRAPPED LIFE-STYLE THEY SEE AROUND THEM."

VIVIENNE WESTWOOD'S LONDON

The life and career of Vivienne, the quintessential British fashion designer, was shaped in London. From founding the punk movement to being a national treasure with a damehood, she is as significant to the city as royal palaces and red post boxes. Here are the London spots that shaped her life, her business and her provocative spirit.

HARROW

In 1958, when Vivienne was 17, her parents bought the post office at 31 Station Road in what is now the London Borough of Harrow, and the family moved from Derbyshire to live in a flat above the shop. Her early creativity was shaped by this time in the north-west of the capital, as she enrolled at Harrow Art School, also on Station Road, and immersed herself in the local mod culture.

After dropping out of college, she found a job at the Kodak Works manufacturing plant, just a short walk from her home. And following her marriage in 1962, she and husband Derek Westwood moved into a terraced house at 86 Station Road.

PORTOBELLO ROAD AND BRICK LANE MARKETS

Vivienne's first foray into trade was in the early '60s, selling her own jewellery at Portobello Road Market, a vibrant hub for unique fashions sold by independent makers and sellers. A few years later, Vivienne and Malcolm would browse the market stalls in the vibrant Brick Lane, in the East End, every Saturday to snap up rock 'n' roll records and clothing, which would then be resold in their first shop, Let It Rock.

AIGBURTH MANSIONS, OVAL

Vivienne and Malcolm McLaren crossed the Thames to south London, when they moved into a ground-floor flat in a Victorian block, Aigburth Mansions, located on Hackford Road, with children Joe and Ben.

THURLEIGH COURT, CLAPHAM

In spring 1969, Vivienne, Malcolm and the children moved to 10 Thurleigh Court, Nightingale Lane, in Clapham, a flat within a 1930s Art Deco building. It was here that punk was conceived, and her early collections were created, as she dyed fabric in the bathtub, cut cloth and operated her sewing machine in the front room to construct designs for her ready-to-wear collections.

THE KING'S ROAD (OPPOSITE LEFT)

Of all the places in London, the King's Road was the birthplace of Vivienne Westwood as provocateur. In the late '60s the thoroughfare on the rougher side of Chelsea was home to some of the most subversive, cutting-edge boutiques that were frequented by achingly cool figures like Mick Jagger. Granny Takes a Trip was at 488 King's Road, and Mr Freedom, glam rock purveyor, was at no. 430. By November 1971, Vivienne and Malcolm had opened their first shop, Let It Rock. A year later it changed to Too Fast to Live Too Young to Die, then SEX in 1974, and in December 1976 it became Seditionaries, the centre of punk. By 1980, the shop had been transformed into Worlds End, where the Pirate collection was sold.

ST CHRISTOPHER'S PLACE, NEAR OXFORD STREET

In March 1982, Vivienne and Malcolm opened a second shop, Nostalgia of Mud, on St Christopher's Place, a narrow, low-key street just off bustling Oxford Street. The opening of this short-lived venture coincided with the launch of their new collection with

the same title, but also known as Buffalo. Designed to resemble an archaeological dig, it featured a 3-D map of the world on the outside, tarpaulin and scaffolding on the inside, and a pool of bubbling mud.

PILLAR HALL, OLYMPIA EXHIBITION CENTRE

Before the launch of London Fashion Week in 1984, designers exhibited their collections at the British Designer Show, which was held at Olympia Exhibition Centre, a glass-ceilinged space in Hammersmith dating from 1886. In 1981, Vivienne showed her first collection, Pirate, in the classical Pillar Hall, with its ornate stucco and Corinthian pillars.

OLD TOWN, CLAPHAM

In 2000, Vivienne moved out of the Thurleigh Court flat that had been her home since 1970, and into an historic 1703 brick Queen Anne house, which she shared with husband Andreas. She adored working in the garden, and browsing her books on her crammed bookshelves, which inspired a fabric print in the Spring/Summer 2001 collection.

DAVIES STREET, MAYFAIR (ABOVE)

In December 1990, Vivienne was able to open a high-end boutique, Vivienne Westwood, on Davies Street, Mayfair. It was a sign of a change in fortunes for her label, now located in one of the most prestigious areas of London. The boutique at 6 Davies Street is now a bespoke Vivienne Westwood bridal couture service.

BATTERSEA

In 1992, Vivienne opened her new studio in Battersea, in a former school building on Elcho Street which she converted into offices and workrooms. She cycled there every day from her home in Clapham; a journey that took 15 minutes. Just as the studio underwent an architectural transformation, the opening of the Royal College of Art, Design and Innovation Campus introduced a flood of creativity to the area, and the Autumn/Winter 2022–3 collection was designed as a celebration of Battersea and its vibrancy.

4

NEW WAVE PIRATES

After punk imploded with the death of Sid Vicious, Vivienne was unsure of her next direction. She hadn't considered herself a fashion designer; rather, it was something she had picked up because of Malcolm, and she was also self-taught, having honed her craft "messing about with Butterick patterns".[71]

But when she saw how much her designs were influencing the Paris catwalk, or the safety pins and rips of designers such as Zandra Rhodes, she realized: "I'd be stupid not to make some money out of it."[72] Vivienne, as a passionate researcher, came across a book on nineteenth-century fashions, and she was drawn to the images and descriptions of a resistance subculture of the French Revolution era. In the aftermath of the Terror, a rebellious group of young royalists wore the exaggerated fashions of the now extinct court of Louis XVI, and like punk, "all its promise of change, and its violence and sexiness" was thrilling.

The men were known as *les Incroyables*, and the women as *les Merveilleuses*, and they used fashion to signal their individuality and their resistance to the new republic and its promotion of the "sans culotte" style. It was all very surreal – *les Incroyables* exaggerated the "macaroni" dandy with trousers that were too short, bicorn hats and cravats pulled up over their necks, wigs and coats back to front, and hair brushed forward and shaved at the neck, as if prepped for the guillotine.

Les Merveilleuses went for the undressed look, with their transparent neoclassical gowns that nodded to the democracies of ancient Greece and Rome, and which they wetted so that they clung to the body. It was an early anti-fashion movement that used non-verbal signals to resist the norm, and which used

OPPOSITE Vivienne, Malcolm and models wearing the Savage collection for Spring/Summer 1982, at the Worlds End shop.

LEFT Cover for *The Merveilleuses Lancers*, melodies by Hugo Felix, arranged by Leonard Williams, 1906.

OPPOSITE Steve Strange and Julia at The Blitz Club in Covent Garden, London, 1980.

humour in the face of devastation. At "victims' balls", they wore red ribbons around their throats, as if they had been decapitated.

The hairstyles for both men and women were very similar to the one sported by Rod Stewart and the mod revival, but when she showed her ideas to Malcolm, his immediate reaction was that young people wouldn't get it. Instead, he suggested that they reject punk's nihilistic black in favour of bright colours, and that they take on the image of pirates, whose swagger would capture the youthful imagination of a new street style that was emerging in London in the aftermath of punk.

Every Tuesday, an eccentric crowd of art students and former punks gathered at the Covent Garden basement wine bar Blitz, where, with a flair for gender fluidity, they wore their own homemade outré fashions with exaggerated make-up. They were eighteenth-century fops, futuristic Teddy boys, Pierrots and Jacobites, and they were setting the new rules of street style, which was exactly the type of escapism that was needed following years of discontent. They typically selected unisex, fantasy pieces from Helen Robinson's PX boutique in Covent Garden. After opening in 1978, this became the premier place for club-goers to buy adapted military wear and velvet suits with frilly white blouses. At first, they were known as the Blitz Kids, but then another moniker would be created – the New Romantics.

BLIT
OCKTAILS
95

"THEY DIDN'T WANT TO CUT A TROUSER THAT NEATLY DEFINED THE TWO CHEEKS OF YOUR BUM. THEY WERE INTERESTED IN SEXUALITY IN A TOTALLY DIFFERENT WAY."

All of this would be the inspiration that Vivienne tapped into as she designed what would become known as the Pirate collection. She searched costume archives to analyse the historical construction of clothing. Just as she had picked apart Teddy boy suits and deconstructed T-shirts, she was fascinated by the original cut of the eighteenth century, and she found that rather than being cut to fit the body, they were draped. When she came across an engraving of a pirate in trousers that were too big and loose around the crotch, she was inspired to replicate this rakishness. "They didn't want to cut a trouser that neatly defined the two cheeks of your bum," she said. "They were interested in sexuality in a totally different way."[73]

A particular source of inspiration were the diagrams of ethnic tailoring in Max Tilke's book *Costume Patterns and Designs*, and what impressed her was the way that rectangles of fabric were used to minimize waste. There was a nod to Native American traditional dress, and as she looked to the pirates of the eighteenth century, she was also drawn to the Hollywood swashbucklers like Errol Flynn.

Black had been the predominant colour for punk, as, according to Malcolm it spoke of "Nihilism. Boredom. Emptiness". But now the Pirate collection would be striking in its colour, with cottons inspired by the dyes from the African Gold Coast, of saffron, cobalt, chrome yellow, vermilion and lapis lazuli.[74] There were graphic patterns from African (or Dutch) wax printed textiles which resembled ropes; striped calf-length trousers trimmed with lace, jackets opened to reveal the stomach, loose blouses and scarves tied around the waist, and Neoclassical translucent white gowns. For Vivienne, her creations were designed to lift spirits in the face of economic depression. "I want to feel rich. And pirates combine toughness with romance and the heroism I admire."[75] She also saw it as an answer to the impending technological age of the '80s, where "we need to equip ourselves with a feeling of human warmth from past ages – of culture taken from the time of pirates and Louis XIV."[76] With its imagery of highwaymen, Robin Hood, pirates, and the expressiveness of youth, it was heroic, powerful and rebellious.

During this period, Vivienne had also softened her own image from the hard-edged dominatrix to a scrubbed, make-up-free

ABOVE A Worlds End clothing label, 1981.

ABOVE Jordan and Steve Severin in the Worlds End shop in 1981, wearing clothing from the Pirate collection.

appearance, and with her henna-tinted hair worn in plaits. Her clothing was now soft and layered; romantic rather than sexual. The physical relationship between Malcolm and Vivienne came to an end in 1979 when he left her to move in with a German designer, Andrea Linz. Even though their relationship had been marked by arguments and detachment, she was in emotional agony at the rejection. For the next four years she felt "dead inside" and that she was just "burning with betrayal; somehow, having invested so much pain in the relationship, that's what it was about."[77] As a support, her friend Gene Krell moved into her home as a lodger, and she continued to create, dying fabrics in the bathtub, silk-screen printing on the living-room table, and experimenting with calicos as she draped and cut.

In 1979, with the shop now boarded up, there was much anticipation as to what the new incarnation could be. Malcolm settled on The Worlds End, taking its name from both its location in a part of the King's Road known as the World's End, and from the satirical William Hogarth print *The Bathos* (1764). It depicts the wilted figure of Time among ruins, including a shop sign, "The World's End", hanging over him. Malcolm's vision for the shop was to have a concept of challenging time, and so he displayed two clocks with 13-hour faces that also ran backwards.[78]

When it reopened in autumn 1980, former punks, New Romantics and fashion journalists all clamoured to see this new look. They were particularly impressed by the Errol Flynn

"PUNK IS OUT, PIRATES AND SWASHBUCKLING ROMANCE ARE IN."

The *Observer*

shirts and high-necked jackets, and the "cleverly cut trousers", as described by Liz Smith in the *Evening Standard* in November 1980. "The elaborate shackles of the punks are about to be thrown off, it seems," she wrote. "The colourful spiky crewcut of the sales girls like Jordan have been growing out and even that grand Dame of Punk has a head of ringlets curled with rags and a few goldbraided pigtails. Their healthier looking bronze make-up is an improvement on scary white and pink masks."[79]

"Punk is out, pirates and swashbuckling romance are in," agreed the *Observer* in January 1981. "And leading the way back to dramatic dressing of a softer sort are two of the leading exponents of chains, punks and bondage ... At the revamped World's End, the new clothes are piratical, dashing and extremely versatile. You can either go the whole hog, even to the pirate's hat, or you can simply buy one of the giant cotton shirts and wear it with a pair of plain trousers."[80]

Musician Adam Ant hired Malcolm to help him transform the aesthetics of his band, Adam and the Ants, who had emerged from the punk scene and had initially been managed by Jordan. He became one of the first to be kitted out by Vivienne as a swashbuckler. As he told journalist Michael Watts: "I'm sick of this new Puritanism there's been in England since '76 ... I like a bit of color, a bit of flash, a bit of honor, a bit of dash."[81]

At the same time as Vivienne was honing the fashion, Malcolm was looking for a new band to manage. "I used to be looked down upon in the music industry," he reflected in 1995. "'You're nothing but a cheap haberdasher on the King's Road,' I was told. 'What do you know about music?' This was meant to be derogatory, of course. But I was thrilled to be a haberdasher. Somehow, I guess because of the success of punk rock, because of the Sex Pistols and their alliance with my store, it became important for a group to be dressed correctly, and that happened at the beginning of the 80's."[82]

After being asked by Adam Ant to manage his band, Malcolm ousted him as lead singer, recruited a 13-year-old singer, Annabella Lwin, and renamed them Bow Wow Wow. He was using the band as a front for his support of pirate radio stations and the new threat to the music industry, recordable cassette tapes, and they were to be the perfect representation for the Pirate look, blending fashion and art with new wave and worldbeat music.

ABOVE Bow Wow Wow lead singer Annabella Lwin with Vivienne Westwood in 1980, wearing pieces from the Pirate collection.

To herald a new era where Vivienne was now considering herself a fashion designer for the first time, they decided to bring their collection to the catwalk. Their first fashion show was held in March 1981 at the Pillar Hall, in the Olympia Exhibition Centre. An audience including Mick Jagger, Adam Ant, Boy George, and art and fashion scenesters watched with fascination as the models paraded out to the sound of Bow Wow Wow. The models were given a ragtag of different hairstyles as they danced down the catwalk in the soft, layered clothing, and make-up artist Yvonne Gold, who had been a teenage customer at Let It Rock, covered their teeth with gold foil from cigarette packets. At the opening of her exhibition at the V&A in 2004, Vivienne called the Pirate collection the crucible of her style and technique. "With that collection, I realized what I could do with ethnic and historical cutting."[83]

Blitz had closed in October 1980, but the kids from the club were now entering into music, with Spandau Ballet's first single, 'To Cut a Long Story Short', coming out at the end of that month, and Steve Strange's band Visage releasing 'Fade to Grey' shortly after. These new wave bands brought the spirit and look of Pirate to their performances, further helping it go mainstream. "Clothes for heroes" had been printed on the labels at Seditionaries and this idea was carried into the new romantics, with Blitz host Steve Strange opening a new night, Club for

Heroes. "We're making people realize that Britain has got something happening again which has been missing, I think anyway," he said in 1982. When Adam Ant released his single 'Stand and Deliver' in May 1981, dressed as a swaggering highwayman, the look was now the defining aesthetic of the British new wave.

The Pirate collection was shown six months before the wedding of Lady Diana Spencer and Prince Charles, with a bridal gown that was the ultimate princess confection of voluminous layers of silk taffeta and lace. This new romanticism caught on with the Sloane Rangers and Chelsea set who copied Diana's wardrobe of foppish blouses with bows, lace and pie-crust collars; the type of blouse that had been shown by Vivienne with Pirate.

In August 1981, British *Vogue* carried a four-page feature on Pirate, as it celebrated the romantic takeover of London. The editorial was selected and styled by Grace Coddington, who followed the unisex ethos and accessorized the loose blouses with Fair Isle knits. This collection, with its bright colours and

BELOW Pirate boots on the catwalk in 1981.

"WITH THAT COLLECTION, I REALIZED WHAT I COULD DO WITH ETHNIC AND HISTORICAL CUTTING."

soft layering, was much more accessible to fashion journalists and buyers than the deliberate confrontation of punk, and the fashion buyer at Bloomingdales even bought some pieces.[84] Valerie Mendes from the V&A had a sense of its importance, and with great foresight, snapped up an outfit for the museum's permanent collection.

The success of this first collection helped Vivienne to realize that she needed to distance herself from Malcolm, and that her fashion should be a separate entity from his music. It was at this point that she saw her future as a designer, whereas previously, her interests were tied with street culture. What she had hit upon, with some guidance from Malcolm, was a theatrical, gender-fluid mode of dress that would continue to make an impact over the next decade and beyond. "It's a look that has gone all over the place, reached into theatre and film," she proudly stated decades later. "You can see it in *Pirates of the Caribbean*, even: Jack Sparrow could have been on the Pirates catwalk."[85]

Despite the antagonism between Vivienne and Malcolm, they continued to collaborate, with the next direction focusing on Malcolm's world music and hip-hop, and her fascination with anthropology. Savage, for Spring/Summer 1982, took inspiration from the pages of *National Geographic* as Vivienne studied the simplicity of ethnic dress, and borrowed the cut of Japanese costume. Rather than Yves Saint Laurent's approach to ethnic dress with his North African, Russian and Chinese-infused collections made to Western tastes, she wanted authenticity, where the incorporation of found items and recycling were the antithesis of consumerism.[86]

Savage was shown at Olympia in October 1981, and models cavorted down the catwalk in vivid colours and striped fabrics, with painted symbols on their bare legs, and with jersey tops that were pulled low and then raised as they walked. She called it a "suppression and release of garments". There were Peruvian hats and Aztec designs, which Malcolm mixed with neon stripes inspired by the Adidas sportswear of hip-hop. He tapped into David Lynch's cult movie *The Elephant Man* (1980), with Foreign Legion hats worn backwards and with eyeholes cut into them. The collection was also infused with modern art, as models opened their togas to reveal Picasso's *Guernica* and *Weeping Woman*, and Andy Warhol's *Campbell's Soup Cans*.[87]

OPPOSITE Model and singer Nick Kamen on the runway at the Pirate show, held at Olympia on 22 October 1981.

CLOCKWISE FROM TOP RIGHT The Pirate collection, shown in London on 3 April 1981, featured Grecian cotton dresses, foppish blouses with rope print fabric, striped trousers and double-breasted jackets.

LEFT Vivienne and Mclaren's Worlds End Savage collection, 1981.

OPPOSITE Malcolm and Vivienne in 1981.

Malcolm returned to New York to find a support act for Bow Wow Wow in the downtown hip-hop clubs, and immersed in the sound, he was inspired to bring the DJ techniques of scratching back to the UK. His single 'Buffalo Gals', released in November 1982, was the soundtrack to their new Buffalo collection for Autumn/Winter 1982. It was officially known as Nostalgia of Mud, named after their new shop at St Christopher's Place, near Oxford Street, which had opened in March. The shop's fitter, Roger K. Burton, who had previously designed the PX and Worlds End boutiques, was given a brief of mud, Peruvian women and scratch music to create the illusion of an architectural dig, with a collapsed floor, a cracked lava floor and the effect of bubbling mud.

Instead of the bright oversized layers of Pirate, Buffalo had a muted palette of browns and greens, rust and dusty pink, because, said Vivienne, "I was really into dyeing at that stage, to make life shine through the dullness of the colour." As a comment about culture and technology in the post-industrial age, and to go back to earlier societies, Vivienne juxtaposed South American ethnic dress, of Bolivian skirts, muddy felts and baby-sling bags, with contemporary North American styles such as the soon-to-be

ABOVE American hip-hop radio show duo The World's Famous Supreme Team, and model Herbie Mensah, all wearing items from Westwood's Buffalo collection, London, February 1983. McLaren and the Supreme Team had recently had a hit single together with 'Buffalo Gals'.

OPPOSITE The Autumn/Winter 1982 Buffalo collection featured sheepskin jackets, dirndl skirts and the buffalo hat.

cult buffalo hats, while the black kohl stripes on the eyes were borrowed from the replicants in the 1982 film *Blade Runner*.[88]

Vivienne credited Malcolm with the concept of underwear as outerwear, by placing a 1950s-styled satin bra over blouses and hooded tops, and teaming them with low-slung dirndl skirts and slouchy heeled boots. This look had been inspired by the women in black South African townships who showed off Western lingerie over their clothes, and after its appearance in Buffalo, Jean Paul Gaultier would transform it into a commercial enterprise with his designs for Madonna in the early '90s.

After the first show at the Pillar Hall in London on 24 March 1982, Nostalgia of Mud was shown in Paris five days later at the Art Nouveau tearoom Angelina on the Rue de Rivoli. Make-up artist Yvonne Gold remembered the activity behind the scenes at Angelina's, where Vivienne's friends and family all chipped in to help amid the chaos, and that she had only seven minutes per face, for a "two-toned rose and peach freshly fucked flush blush with mascara-less (unheard of) moody, hollowed eyes". As the models made their way down the spiral staircase to the sound of Malcolm's hip-hop, Paris's fashion buyers and the press didn't know what to make of it.[89]

While they took only £500 in orders, the Buffalo collection, like so many of Vivienne's designs, would influence other designers, particularly in Japan, with Rei Kawakubo of Comme des Garçons and Yohji Yamamoto drawn to replicating the baggy layering and muted palettes for their own collections. It also

"I KNEW BY THEN THAT I HAD A TALENT, A CONFIDENCE GIVEN IN PART BY THE FACT THAT I'D SEEN ALL THIS PUNK STUFF THAT I HAD ORIGINATED BEING SHOWN ON PARIS CATWALKS."

filtered onto the high street, but this cultural success didn't help to pay the rent on their shops. The situation was made worse when it was discovered that Worlds End manager Michael Collins had been taking cash and stock to support his heroin habit; given how chaotic the till system was, it had gone unnoticed.

The new Spring/Summer 1983 collection, known as Punkature, and nicknamed "bag lady chic", was shown in October 1982 at the Louvre Palace. Vivienne's vision was to redefine ugly and beautiful, and the collection was a futuristic update of punk, where rough stitching, hand-dyed and distressed fabrics, and the use of recycling and upcycling before those terms existed, helped create an unfinished vibe. Cardigans were studded with large buttons from tin-can lids, and shoes were inspired by the makeshift sandals worn in Brazilian favelas, which were constructed from tires and cord. It was here that she also introduced one of her most groundbreaking inventions, the tube skirt; a jersey tube that could be worn around the body and pulled up or down for different lengths. She had come up with the concept when playing with tubes of double stockinette that were sold as window cleaning fabric. Having already used household products for her "kitchen sink" cardigan, using dishcloth cotton and lids from Vim scouring powder containers to make buttons, she experimented with wearing the stockinette in one piece.[90] As she told *Desert Island Discs* in 1992, "it's really odd to think that nobody actually made a sort of knitted or sweatshirt or jersey sort of skirt before, and I did it because it seemed too obvious."[91]

The Witches collection for Autumn/Winter 1983 was inspired by the 1978 book *Voodoo and Magic Practices*, by Jean Kerboull, a missionary priest in Haiti, and it was fused with the sound and feel of *Duck Rock*, Malcolm's album of hip-hop and African music. Vivienne commissioned New York graffiti artist Keith Haring to create neon hieroglyphics with voodoo and incest imagery as a code of magic symbols. It was a mix of the fitted and the baggy, with layers wrapped tightly or swirling around the body, hoods that looked like witches' hats, the square-cut sleeves of Japanese kimonos, hip-length cardigans with peaked shoulders and sheepskin jackets with toggles. There were also gymslips,

OPPOSITE A coat with kimono sleeves from the Autumn/Winter 1983 Witches collection.

ABOVE Vivienne in her studio in 1983.

as if from her school days, and tube skirts of fluorescent jersey which were worn with oversized trainers. These wedge-heeled, triple-tongued trainers, designed by Patrick Cox and praised by American *Vogue*, were one of the first times a designer had brought sports shoes onto the catwalk.

In 1983, British *Vogue* named Vivienne and Malcolm the "chief engineers of contemporary style", but by then Vivienne was ready to move on from him. "Gradually the confidence began to come back," she said. "Number one, I knew by then that I had a talent, a confidence given in part by the fact that I'd seen all this punk stuff that I had originated being shown on Paris catwalks. I saw how it had changed everything. It had changed hairstyles. It had changed *Vogue*. I could see I was being taken seriously."[92]

Her devastation after the collapse of her relationship with Malcolm McLaren was cured when she met an Italian textile businessman, Carlo D'Amario, around the time of her Witches collection. Five years her junior, they were soon involved in both a physical and professional relationship, and with Carlo shocked that her critical success hadn't translated financially, he persuaded her to come to Italy.

Hypnos, for Spring/Summer 1984, was her last collection with Malcolm, and while his name was on the label, it was designed entirely by Vivienne and made in Italy. Inspired by the first Olympics and named after the Greek god of sleep, it was

ABOVE Vivienne wearing sportswear from the Hypnos collection for Spring/Summer 1984.

loaded with the paganism and sexuality of the ancient Greeks. The phallic symbols, such as penis-shaped buttons and Medusas with penises instead of snakes for hair, led to it being dubbed the "Porno Olympics" collection by *The Face* magazine.[93] The Paris fashion show in October 1983 offered the shock factor, as female models sported jockstraps and kneepads over their tracksuits, and Yvonne Gold smudged silvery-grey make-up around the lips to resemble herpes sores.

While Vivienne was in Italy, and Malcolm was in Hollywood living with actress Lauren Hutton, the two shops were shuttered and neglected. As the bills piled up, and bailiffs threatened to auction their contents, the Worlds End business was dissolved, and Vivienne filed for personal bankruptcy. She was now free from Malcolm, and her last collection under Worlds End would be the Clint Eastwood collection for Autumn/Winter 1984. It was both a spoof of spaghetti westerns, and a tribute to being made in Italy, with fabrics printed with logos from classic Italian brands like Fiat and Olivetti, and it was another contrast between loose and tight, with tube skirts, fluorescent belted macs, and short-legged bondage trousers. Vivienne had become sole designer of her own brand, and even though her innovations would inspire and enrich other designers, she would still struggle for the next ten years to build a profitable business.

PIRATE BOOTS

When Kate Moss wore the original strapped boots from the 1981 Pirate collection to a party in 2001, the paparazzi shots sparked a wave of interest in Vivienne's older collections. Kate had teamed her pirate boots with a denim miniskirt and an old parka, and it was this slouchy aesthetic that sparked a huge fashion revival.

Kate Moss was one of the few celebrities in the 2000s whose every outfit elicited a frenzied mimicry. Her flawless style, of boho festival flair and vintage elegance, was pinned to every designer mood board and drove the fortunes of e-commerce brands. It wasn't just the clothes, it was the way she wore them with just-out-of-bed hair and a rebellious edge that painted an image of a woman always having a good time. The boots proved to be a favourite in her wardrobe, as she had previously rocked them with a black leather jacket, denim skirt and tights in 1999, and as a contrast to delicate underwear while eating a sandwich in a 2000 photo by Corinne Day.

The demand for the boots was now so high that when Vivienne reintroduced them in yellow, brick, brown, black leather and grey suede, there was an extensive waiting list.[94] *Harper's Bazaar* called it a "typical which-came-first story: Vivienne Westwood's decision to reintroduce her buckle-laden pirate boots or the Kate Moss sighting."[95]

Sienna Miller was spotted wearing them at Coachella Music festival in 2008, but they would be linked forever with Kate. She was photographed wearing different versions of the boot over the years, and in June 2016, a 42-year-old Kate once again revived the pirate boots when she was spotted in London with Naomi Campbell.

ABOVE Kate Moss leaving Nobu restaurant in London, wearing a fur coat and Westwood pirate boots, 10 November 2009.

OPPOSITE Moss wearing vintage Westwood pirate boots in Soho, London, 15 June 2016.

5

THE ARISTOCRATIC EDGE

OPPOSITE Vivienne with her son Joseph Corré in a 1985 portrait.

Having spent a year in Italy, absorbing the culture, the style and the craftmanship, and finally feeling appreciated by the country's fashion press, Vivienne was particularly excited by the news of a potentially lucrative collaboration. In January 1985, D'Amario had successfully orchestrated a deal with Sergio Galeotti, Giorgio Armani's business partner, for the Armani group to produce and distribute her collections. It had sounded almost too good to be true and sadly, when Sergio Galeotti died of an AIDS-related illness, Armani cancelled it in his grief.

Invitations had already been sent out for her new collection, and she was forced to stand outside the tents at the Louvre to personally apologize to her guests that the show was now cancelled. "And I tried to sue Giorgio Armani, but I don't know what happened with that," she said in 1992.[96]

This Italian collection would have included her revolutionary reinterpretation of the Victorian-era crinoline, a creation that would become one of her most impactful and groundbreaking. Instead, thanks to a rescue loan from D'Amario, she launched it separately as the Mini-Crini collection for Spring/Summer 1986. When it was shown at her October 1985 show at the Louvre, it earned praise for its girlish, light feel that was a contrast to the '80s power suits and keep-fit aesthetic. "People want to be able to move more freely now," she said in 1986. "And who knows, maybe someday Linda Evans [from *Dynasty*] will be wearing crinoline."[97]

"PEOPLE WANT TO BE ABLE TO MOVE MORE FREELY NOW."

She had been inspired by the doll in the ballet *Petrushka*, and a photo of the late Queen Elizabeth as a little girl, to create bell-shaped skirts printed with stars and spots, like Minnie Mouse, and

LEFT Sara Stockbridge in the mini-crini for Spring/Summer 1985.

OPPOSITE A model on the catwalk for the Mini-Crini collection.

which were worn with platform shoes that featured wooden soles – the first showing of her rocking horse shoes. After the pain of having her contract with Armani cancelled, she had come back swinging. "I have every intention of being successful," she told *Women's Wear Daily* in January 1986, "because when I die I'll feel very stupid if I never did what I really wanted … What I've got in my hand as far as business is very little, but I've gotten a lot clearer in my head."[98]

While her balletic take on the crinoline and the miniskirt kick-started a trend for puffball skirts, it wasn't she who profited from it. Instead, it was Christian Lacroix and Karl Lagerfeld for Chanel who had reinterpreted it to great success by autumn 1986. As fashion journalist Jane Procter wrote in the *Evening Standard* in October 1986: "The short balletic skirt has a mixed parentage. Vivienne Westwood with her mini-crinolines was the

LEFT Vivienne poses for a portrait in New York, in 1986.

acknowledged mother, but the paternity is disputed between Christian Lacroix and his bouncing bubbles for Patou couture and Jean Paul Gaultier, with his ruffled balloons."[99]

A few years later, she was asked why it took so long for her to be a financial success, when so many of her ideas were copied by other fashion houses. She believed it was because her designs were considered uncommercial and had to be adjusted and "watered down" by others. "It's just that they're new so it sometimes takes a little longer for people's eye, or sentiments, to get used to," she said.[100]

She returned to London to face the huge debts from the Worlds End business with Malcolm. Nostalgia of Mud had been forced to close, and because she had signed for personal bankruptcy, her mother, Dora, and son Joseph were named as directors of Casnell Ltd, a new company for her brand. She unlocked the doors to

"IT IS IMPORTANT, I THINK, TO GET MY CLOTHES SEEN AROUND AND IT WILL REALLY HELP ME TO REFINE THE DESIGNS. IT WILL LET ME SEE HOW PEOPLE WEAR MY CLOTHES BEFORE THEY ARE FOR SALE ALL OVER."

Worlds End, reconnected the water and gas supply, and after a thorough clean-up of the space, she was ready to open it in July 1986, with the rails stocked with the mini-crini. "I intend to use it to sell prototypes of my collections a year before they are available elsewhere," she told *Women's Wear Daily* at the time. "It is important, I think, to get my clothes seen around and it will really help me to refine the designs. It will let me see how people wear my clothes before they are for sale all over."[101]

Her year in Milan had imprinted on her the immense beauty of art and historic costume, but now that she was back in London, she was feeling even more appreciative of English tailoring and aristocratic elegance. She told *Women's Wear Daily* that she found Savile Row much more interesting than the King's Road, as she purposefully shifted from the anarchic layering and punky youth ethos of previous collections. She was particularly passionate about reviving the traditional textile crafts which had suffered under modern machinery. Hardy fabrics were a vital component of upper-class dress – good quality tweed jackets that passed down the generations and were worn for field sports, the Fair Isle sweaters like those of the Duke of Windsor, the wool tartan in the family's sett – and so Harris tweed, once the bastion of aristo-sports style, became a focus. The rough wool fabric, still traditionally made by Outer Hebrides crofters, had been named a protected cloth when the Harris Tweed Association (later the Harris Tweed Authority) was established in 1909. Reams of cloth were stamped with the Orb Mark to indicate they had been spun, dyed and hand-woven on the islands of Harris and Lewis.

She spent the winter of 1986 researching this next Harris Tweed collection for Autumn/Winter 1987. She considered all the rules of aristocratic dress, that there was a type of jacket for fox hunting and one for grouse shooting, and "I thought of debutantes going to balls but with a Barbour jacket flung over their ballgown; that mix, that ease with chic and tradition."[102]

Vivienne's manufacturing process was very different from the other fashion houses whose lines were produced on a larger scale in factories. Working like a cottage industry, she hand-cut and stitched the fabric on her domestic sewing machine on the table in her living room in Thurleigh Court, working with single-width traditional tweed, rather than the double-width on industrial cutting machines.[103]

ABOVE Vivienne wearing the tweed crown, regal cape and pearls with orb from the Harris Tweed collection in 1987.

OPPOSITE A pink lambswool twinset, multiple strings of pearls and a checked wool mini-crini from the Harris Tweed collection.

It was during this time that she came up with the Vivienne Westwood orb logo, which bore a startling similarity to the trademarked Harris Tweed stamp of authenticity. She insisted that the symbol came to her while designing a sweater that she could imagine Prince Charles wearing with a kilt. Her son Ben was interested in astronomy, and with all his books lying around the house, she was struck by the visuals of the orb as a ringed planet, resembling Saturn.[104] "I have the tradition of the orb, which is what the Queen holds in her hand, and I've launched it into space," she said. "That's who I feel I am."[105] It was a fitting reference to her moniker as the "Queen of Punk", although eyebrows were raised that she had lifted the Harris Tweed orb and Maltese cross for her own purposes. In the 1990s, the Harris Tweed Authority began legal proceedings against Vivienne for infringing on their logo, but they were able to come to an agreement.

The Harris Tweed collection combined her appreciation of the eccentricity of the upper classes, her parodying of aspects of the royal family, and the eroticism she found in the buttoned-up schoolteacher or nanny, which also harked back to how Malcolm had styled her in the '60s. She was inspired by the society pages of *Tatler*; the posh debutantes in their pearls and sweaters who appeared to be good girls, but with a naughtiness simmering under the surface.

"I THOUGHT OF DEBUTANTES GOING TO BALLS BUT WITH A BARBOUR JACKET FLUNG OVER THEIR BALLGOWN; THAT MIX, THAT EASE WITH CHIC AND TRADITION."

LEFT Model wearing a Harris Tweed cape and crown in September 1987.

OPPOSITE Models Sara Stockbridge and Patsy Kensit on the catwalk for the Harris Tweed collection in March 1987.

ABOVE Vivienne on the catwalk for the finale of the Harris Tweed collection, October 1987.

ABOVE RIGHT Vivienne with the Love jacket in her new shop, 1988.

OPPOSITE Vivienne poses for a portrait in 1987, wearing the Love Jacket from the Harris Tweed collection.

She studied Norman Hartnell and his designs for the Queen, the matching coats worn by the princesses Elizabeth and Margaret in the '30s, and the twinsets and pearls that the Queen often teamed with a kilt. The manufacturer of these twinsets was John Smedley, whose knitted woollen garments had been made in Matlock, Derbyshire since 1784; and she remembered fondly that they had been sold from her mother's post office in Tintwistle. She visited the Smedley factory in autumn 1986, and with an absolute clarity on what she wanted, she asked for the colours that were considered out-of-date; pale pink, post box red, primrose, taupe, and with buttons branded with the new orb logo. They were also a nod to former sales assistant Jordan, who had worn them with her spiked bleached hair and Mondrian face in Derek Jarman's *Jubilee* (1978).[106]

These twinsets were paired with voluminous mini-crinis, strings of pearls, and with another innovation, her reinvented corset. Nicknamed the "Stature of Liberty" corset, it was based on the eighteenth-century styles of European courts, where they scooped up the breasts into separated, rounded domes. Corsetry would become a fixture of her collections as they pulled in the silhouette and changed the posture, and, like the mini-crini, the "Stature of Liberty" corset would be copied profitably by other designers, including Karl Lagerfeld for Chanel in 1990.

Shown at the Olympia Exhibition Centre for London Fashion Week in March 1987, it was her first London show without Malcolm. Whereas he had always promoted his own new wave and hip-hop, she chose to have her models walk in front of the orb logo backdrop to classical music; Tchaikovsky's Sleeping Beauty, Debussy, and 'My Love Is Like a Red, Red Rose', played by a Yorkshire brass band. Yet there were also comedic touches with her models made up to look like drunken *Tatler* girls, their lipstick smeared from kissing boyfriends, and their messy hair topped with colourful tweed crowns by milliner Stephen Jones.

"SUDDENLY, WE HAD THIS DESIGN ICON USE HARRIS TWEED WHEN IT HAD PREVIOUSLY BEEN RESERVED FOR OUR DAD'S JACKETS ... VIVIENNE MOVED IT INTO THESE WILD COLOUR SCHEMES."

Lorna Macaulay,
Harris Tweed Authority

It was the era of the Duchess of York bringing jolly humour and brassiness to the royal family, and Vivienne's favourite model, Sara Stockbridge, would epitomize this sauciness. Sara combined a Marilyn Monroe sexiness with a couture elegance, and she resembled a St Trinian's schoolgirl as she opened the show with Vivienne's son Joe, both dressing on stage as "city gents", in striped trousers and black velvet jackets. The models had gorged on alcohol backstage, and so Patsy Kensit tottered unsteadily as her tweed crown slipped from her head and she struggled with the white spotted fur cape around her shoulders. Sadie Frost provocatively opened her blue Harris tweed Princess coat to reveal a tulle ballet skirt and "Stature of Liberty" corset, which sent the photographers into a frenzy.

Despite, or because of, the surrealness of seeing drunken, lipstick-smeared models balancing on their rocking horse shoes, the collection wowed the press, with the *Observer* praising Vivienne for shaking off "the spinster associations of Harris Tweed".[107] It also instigated a fashion revival for the industry, as other designers now sought out what had been considered a staid, old-fashioned textile. Lorna Macaulay, chief executive of the Harris Tweed Authority, said: "Suddenly, we had this design icon use Harris Tweed when it had previously been reserved for our dad's jackets, for Sunday best, and always in these neutral tones. Vivienne moved it into these wild colour schemes, particularly for the tartans and checks. She was always push, push, push for these very vibrant colours." Along with a group of designers that included Bill Gibb, Vivienne visited the Outer Hebrides in the late 1980s to meet Ian Angus Mackenzie, now chief executive at Harris Tweed Hebrides, at his weaving shed in Vatisker on the Isle of Lewis. As Lorna said, "I can only imagine that these conversations with the mill designers would have been like a breath of fresh air for them. At this time, our business was held up by our three button men's sports jacket, which is still an incredibly important part of what we do. But in those days, the designers would have welcomed that edge she brought."[108]

Vivienne posed for photographer Michael Roberts for a spread in British *Vogue* in August 1987, regal in her fur-lined cape and tweed crown, and captured dancing in the ballerina rocking horse shoes, which she credited with changing the posture and for being "so comfortable: they lengthen your stride." Model Sara Stockbridge, earning her own publicity as Vivienne's muse, was featured on the cover of *i-D* magazine in August 1987. Winking to the camera in the tweed crown and cape, the cover line declared, "Vivienne Westwood crowns her princess." Sara had first been hired by Vivienne as a model for the Mini-Crini collection, and soon after she was courted by the designer to be the face of a new pop group, which Vivienne hoped would draw in a younger audience.

BELOW Malcolm offers congratulations to Vivienne after her Harris Tweed show in 1987.

"I'd like to find a girl to sing it, then another and another. And I'd like the girls to stand for different qualities that I believe in, like in 'Masters of the Universe,'" she said in 1986.[109] She named the group Choice, because it sounded democratic and international, and she was ambitious enough to think that Madonna might front the band, after hearing the singer had professed admiration for her. But unable to reach her, she turned to Sara Stockbridge.[110]

"I HAVE THE TRADITION OF THE ORB, WHICH IS WHAT THE QUEEN HOLDS IN HER HAND, AND I'VE LAUNCHED IT INTO SPACE … THAT'S WHO I FEEL I AM."

Like the Sex Pistols, the band would fuse music, fashion and art, and Sara, with her London accent and wink-wink cheekiness, represented the type of Englishness that Vivienne enjoyed playing with. Vivienne wrote their songs, including 'Bride of Fortune', and the band toured venues across the country in 1988 in collaboration with *i-D* magazine, while Sara performed in a series of costumes from the collections. "Vivienne's the brains behind it," said Sara in 1988. "She wrote songs for the Sex Pistols and she writes the words and tunes for all these. She already had the band together when she found me. She said 'Can you sing Sarah?' so I said 'Oooh, I can try.'"[111]

The smudgy lipstick had become a trademark for Sara, and made it into a lyric from the song which implied she woke up to find someone kissing her. Looking back on the inappropriateness of the lyrics through a modern eye, Sara laughed to *Dazed Digital*, "But Vivienne wouldn't give a fuck about that. 'Ooh, whatcha mean? No, don't be stupid!'"

After the success of Harris Tweed, Vivienne decided to upgrade to her own studio, and thanks to a security from fashion designer Jeff Banks, she was able to rent a warehouse in Greenland Street, off Camden High Street. Her employees included Bella Freud and Ben's girlfriend Yasmine Eslami, both of whom would become designers themselves, but her offices were a chaotic mess of fabrics and papers, in stark contrast to the sleek luxury of rival design houses. Yet it would be this way of working that suited her, as she continually pushed to achieve her desire – to be the great British fashion designer.

OPPOSITE Vivienne with her muse, Sara Stockbridge (r), in 1991.

ABOVE A model walks in the Vivienne Westwood Spring/ Summer 1985 Ready-to-Wear show in London. This was known as the Mini-Crini collection.

THE MINI-CRINI

With her take on the crinoline, one of the most controversial of women's fashions from the 1860s, Vivienne's mini-crini offered a new silhouette that was at odds with the structured shoulders and narrow hips that dominated '80s power dressing.

Instead, her combination of Victorian crinoline and '60s youthquake miniskirt was designed to bring freedom and comfort to a coquettish style. "It just collapses around you, so you don't even notice it," she said. "You could sit on a tube train and not really know you've got one on until you get up and it just bells out."

The crinoline had first been popularized by Empress Eugénie of France, the most fashion-forward woman of the mid-nineteenth century, where a cage constructed from steel hoops acted as a canvas for reams of vivid fabrics and elaborate decorations. The crinoline was bulky and cumbersome, yet it was also freeing, as the legs now had room to breathe underneath the stiff birdcage-like structure, while the hoops bobbed around her. Initially a fashion for the upper classes, the style soon caught on with working-class women who bought cheaper versions to emulate a high-status fashion.

Vivienne's mini-crini was born from a combination of influences and loves, from the pictures of Queen Elizabeth as a princess, to a playful 1950s Brigitte Bardot. She had been particularly struck by the ballerinas on stage in the Diaghilev ballet *Petrushka*, and the "little bell-like cut-off crinoline, that swung. I knew that was brilliant. And I saved that idea for a rainy day. And that rainy day came in Italy."[112]

Her Paris show in October 1985 had three different designs to her mini-crini – a pannier, a sphere and a beehive with hoops on the outside. They had a girlish Minnie Mouse aesthetic with the polka-dot and star prints, round-toe platform shoes, and, according to Vivienne, the look of "an old prostitute pretending to be fourteen years old".

ABOVE Woman in bonnet, mantelet cape and wide crinoline dress attending the picture exhibition at the Paris Salon, 1865. Handcoloured lithograph by R.V. after an illustration by Francois Courboin from Octave Uzanne's *Fashion in Paris*, William Heinemann, London, 1898.

The mini-crini was a complete shift in silhouette, and it caused a sensation, but Vivienne wasn't the designer who ultimately profited from it. Instead, Christian Lacroix launched his version, the puffball skirt, which was one of the great, but brief, fashion successes of the mid-1980s. But Vivienne would continue to use the mini-crini and the crinoline concept for later collections.

6

FROM PAGAN TO PORTRAIT

OPPOSITE Vivienne pictured outside her London office in June 1992.

Vivienne's next collection, Britain Must Go Pagan, for Spring/Summer 1988, was the first of a series of five shows that combined the drapery and pagan eroticism of ancient Greece with fine British tailoring. This thread of decadent sexuality and the pursuit of pleasure ran through Britain Must Go Pagan, Time Machine, Civilizade, Voyage to Cythera and Pagan V, for Spring/Summer 1990.

The themes tied in with her fascination with the French Revolution and the pursuit of democracy, as the Regency period, in England, looked to ancient Greece and Rome in the classical cuts of a gown, and the tight riding breeches that promoted an idealized masculine body. Greek statues enhanced the sexuality of the body with defined muscles carved into marble, and she saw the similarities in the eighteenth century, where the men's buff-coloured breeches were worn so tight, they highlighted the genitals.

Sara Stockbridge opened the October 1987 Britain Must Go Pagan show with microphone in hand as she sang her way down the catwalk wearing rocking horse shoes with Hermes wings at the ankles, and a "Centaur" skirt with a flared wool skirt worn over a tight, knee-length jersey. Ancient Greece met British tradition with mini-togas worn with knee-length stockings, tailored jackets and school blazers with the orb logo, and English boater hats. Vivienne had a curious, childlike way of looking at the world, as demonstrated by the schoolboy caps, and while her collection was bursting with historical research and technical skill, she included a corset printed with a Care Bear, one of the most popular children's toys in the late '80s, and galaxies on velvet, as copied from one of Ben's astronomy books.

Vivienne's Autumn/Winter 1988 collection, Time Machine, taking its name from H. G. Wells's 1895 science fiction classic, fully explored the Savile Row tailoring that she was now mimicking and parodying, for both men and women. The show took place in the British Fashion Council tent at Olympia in March 1988, and it was divided into different concepts that traversed British traditions in different time periods. She imagined a young Miss Marple as her central figure, writing in the programme that she was "once a young lady and wore her knockout skirts". Petticoats peeked out from under tweed skirts, and there were draped Greek dresses with corsetry, back-to-front velvet jackets, skirts with lace bustles that looked like a bunny tail, while in a feast of tartan, models broke out into a Highland Fling at the end. *The Sunday Times* concluded that her "use of tradition is ironic but in her enjoyment of it she ends up establishing what she set out to mock."[113]

When she was invited to appear on *Wogan* to show the Time Machine collection, guest host Sue Lawley baited the audience into mocking Vivienne and the "ridiculousness" of her designs. It was the sort of treatment that would be meted out to her by the British media over the next decade, and it was left to Janet Street-Porter, also invited on as a guest, to try to defend her.

If the "Masters of the Universe" sci-fi toy collection had been in her mind when it came to her short-lived pop band Choice, it was also one of the inspirations for her Spring/Summer 1989 Civilizade collection, where she showcased wildly different

ABOVE Harlequin designs from The Voyage to Cythera Autumn/Winter 1989, as shown in the major exhibition of Vivienne's work at the Victoria and Albert Museum, London, 2004.

OPPOSITE LEFT Sara Stockbridge in a draped corset and skirt at the preview of the Spring/Summer 1988 Britain Must Go Pagan collection.

OPPOSITE RIGHT Models on the catwalk for the Spring/Summer 1989 Civilizade collection, part of the Pagan series.

"[SHE] UNVEILED A WOMAN WITH THE FIGURE OF A PAGE THREE GIRL AND THE FASHION PHILOSOPHY OF THE TRUE ANARCHIST."

Rebecca Tyrrel, *The Sunday Times*

ABOVE Vivienne in her fig leaf tights as she joins the picket line at the Natural History Museum in 1990.

"heroes". The name came from a nineteenth-century expression for a desire to influence intellectual development in a society, and here she combined the classics with English traditions, such as the Smedley twinsets, harlequin prints and costumes that resembled rugby jerseys. There was gold lurex and leopard print, draped jersey corsets, including one with pink and brown colour-blocking that reminded her of chocolate wrappers, and a pink gingham apron and jacket, worn over extreme hot pants that revealed a bunny tail, as previously shown in Time Machine. Her show brought London Fashion Week to a close, and, as *The Sunday Times* wrote, she remained "loyal to her favourite fashion characters, unveiled a woman with the figure of a page three girl and the fashion philosophy of the true anarchist. Saris were worn with pink and green fluorescent tulle petticoats. It was the strongest look on the catwalk although it's not likely to be taken up by the majority."[114]

The Voyage to Cythera (Autumn/Winter 1989) collection took its name from Jean-Antoine Watteau's painting of Venus's birthplace, and it was her first collection to be directly inspired by this artist's work, including his depictions of the harlequin from the Italian commedia d'art. It was also an homage to classic Greek statues, with nude bodies eroticized by the drape of fabric, and the sexuality of Regency dress. She studied the men's tight, buff breeches that mimicked the physical perfection of marble gods to create her own versions; harlequin-print sheer bodysuits and flesh-coloured leggings with an artfully placed fig leaf over the crotch to give the illusion of nudity. These leggings, worn with the short Regency-era spencer jacket, were the perfect example of irony and risk-taking, giving a cheeky wink to English prudishness. There were also corsets that revealed nipples, and she brought back the naked breast T-shirts, creating a nostalgic, romantic satire of snobbery.

Some critics were not fans. "The skin-and-bones models who were dressed and undressed, in lurid harlequins, argyles and bodysuits accessorized with the kookiest imaginable collection of sunglasses, shoes and bags bore about as much resemblance to the nudes of classical antiquity as Cher does to Brian Mulroney," wrote the *Toronto Star*'s fashion reporter.[115]

Her argyle leggings, inspired by Léon Bakst's costumes for Diaghilev's *Ballet Russes*, and manufactured by John Smedley,

RIGHT Nadja Auermann walks the catwalk in fig leaf tights at the Spring/Summer 1993 Salon show at Paris Fashion Week in October 1992.

would become bestsellers, while the fig leaf bodysuit would continue to be a jokey reference point in the media to highlight Vivienne's own eccentricity over the next few years. She made a headline-grabbing appearance on *The Dame Edna Experience* in the stockings, and it would cement her in the minds of the public as a risqué provocateur who was the opposite of how a woman approaching 50 should behave.

The final collection in this series of five, Pagan V, was shown in October 1989, but it was poorly received and was a critical and commercial failure. American fashion buyers even walked out at the sight of her cotton separates decorated with phallic symbols that resembled a schoolboy doodle. But there were also striped shirts worn backwards, unisex outfits that resembled pyjamas, and a cow-patterned bodysuit modelled by Sara Stockbridge and inspired by a 1912 Léon Bakst costume for the great dancer Nijinsky. There were also sailors in tank tops printed with HMS

"I'M NOT A FEMINIST ... WHEN WOMEN TRY TO TURN THEMSELVES INTO MEN, IT JUST MAKES FOR MONSTERS LIKE MARGARET THATCHER. FLIRTATION IS A POWER THAT WOMEN SHOULD USE."

ARGO, as a reference to Jason and the Argonauts and their quest for the Golden Fleece.

Women's Wear Daily was more favourable in its review than the walkouts: "Get ready, world: Viv's a Sex Goddess. Her show Monday had its bizarre moments. It began with a girl wearing men's underwear with a large penis printed in the right place ... In between, Westwood showed why she's a designer's designer. She has easy spring jackets, beautiful suits and even if her pants had flies, they were the most feminine in London."[116]

The report also described the show as imprinting the idea of Vivienne as "first impresario of fashion", charging the equivalent of $25 a head for tickets for a second show for a general audience, and like a musician at a rock concert, she was selling her own T-shirts, now branded with penises.[117] However, the orders were so low that it wasn't worth the time of the Italian manufacturers to make them.[118] Despite four years of hard work following her return to London, commercial success, and even financial stability, still eluded Vivienne. "She's like the Queen. She doesn't really understand money," one ex-employee told the *Guardian*.[119] She was so broke, she could only pay people in clothes and was still living in her council house in Clapham. She was regularly spotted cycling across London in her mini-crini and rocking horse shoes, leaving her home with rollers under a scarf if she had an

LEFT Apollo winged rocking horse shoes from the Spring/Summer 1988 Britain Must Go Pagan collection.

ABOVE Sara Stockbridge wearing pieces from the Autumn/Winter 1988 Time Machine collection.

event to attend, or a plastic Vivienne Westwood bag over her head to protect from the rain.[120]

Despite their contrasting politics, Vivienne was often compared to Margaret Thatcher, and to play up to this, photographer and stylist Michael Roberts captured Vivienne's pitch perfect imitation of the prime minister for the April 1989 edition of *Tatler*. With the pearls, the wig and the shoulder-padded suit, she mimicked the expression and pose of Thatcher so thoroughly that it was hard to tell them apart. Vivienne's silhouette was at odds with Thatcher's power dressing, as she preferred the softened shoulders and nipped-in waists of Dior, and she was also not a fan of her politics. "I'm not a feminist. I don't believe in women being like men," she said. "When women try to turn themselves into men, it just makes for monsters like Margaret Thatcher. Flirtation is a power that women should use."[121] While Thatcher never wore Westwood, she was an admirer, particularly when her designs were championed by Romilly McAlpine, the ex-wife of former Conservative Party treasurer Lord McAlpine.

As the Sue Lawley interview had demonstrated, Vivienne was treated as a bit of a joke in Britain rather than being taken seriously for her craft, and the British Fashion Council's Designer of the Year award had so far been elusive. It was also incredibly frustrating to her that John Galliano was the recipient in 1987 and 1988, when she believed that his entire ethos, from his 1983

"THE KEY WORDS ARE DISCRIMINATION AND ELEGANCE, AND THAT'S WHAT A CONSUMER SHOULD REMEMBER WHEN BUYING."

degree show at Central Saint Martins, had been lifted from her Pirate and Buffalo collections.

"I'm the only English designer who's never won the Designer of the Year award. I honestly do not know *why* they do not hold me in the esteem in which they *should* hold me," she told Lynn Barber in February 1990.[122] Some thought that the traditionalists of the fashion council had taken exception to her parodying of the Queen, and that the "God Save the Queen" punk antics were still burned in their mind.

She was given a lifeline when John Fairchild, publisher of *Women's Wear Daily*, named her as one of the six important designers in his autobiography *Chic Savages* in November 1989. He placed her alongside Yves Saint Laurent, Giorgio Armani, Emanuel Ungaro, Karl Lagerfeld and Christian Lacroix, and not only was she the sole woman, but he also described her as the designer's designer. "I do remember Mr Fairchild was the most important person for me in terms of press," she told the *Guardian* in 2001. "Even when I had no collection to speak of, he always was a great supporter. I got this OBE in England, and I think it would never have happened if not for Mr Fairchild. But suddenly, after his remark, the British thought, 'Oh, maybe this madwoman really is a designer.'"[123]

In March 1990, the *Sunday Telegraph* named her as "the most talked about designer in Britain", and in April she was the first fashion designer to be the subject of a documentary for *The South Bank Show*. She was introduced by Melvyn Bragg as "Britain's most influential designer". Despite this (and the John Fairchild comment), the buying public remain baffled by both her and her clothes, which caused discomfort due to her confrontational questioning of sexuality and of beauty.[124]

"In a country in which everyone would prefer to be comfortable, Vivienne Westwood upsets the national equilibrium," wrote the *Guardian* in 1991. "Her appearance doesn't help. From the neck up, she looks like Auntie ... but Auntie wouldn't wear a flesh-coloured bodystocking and wooden rocking horse platforms. A Wogan audience almost laughed themselves silly at her appearance on the show."[125]

In another feature in the *Sunday Telegraph* in March 1990, she was compared to a "Culture-thirsty ex-teacher" and a naïve "little girl" playing with a dressing-up box, and with an image

ABOVE *The Dance* by Jean-Antoine Watteau, French painter in the Baroque and Rococo style, *c.* 1718–21.

ABOVE RIGHT Nadja Auermann in a printed corset and gown in the "Watteau" style, for the Vive la Cocotte Autumn/Winter 1995 collection, shown during Paris Fashion Week.

that juxtaposed the Buckingham Palace establishment with the soap opera *Brookside*. "Ten years on," the article explained, "her lack of personal wealth is at odds with the scale of her reputation and influence. She takes no holidays, lives a celibate life and cycles daily from a cactus-filled purpose-built Clapham flat to her workrooms in Camden Town."[126]

In December 1990, she went to Tokyo for The Fashion Summit 1991, the second annual gathering of international designers, alongside Christian Lacroix, Franco Moschino and Isaac Mizrahi. At a joint press conference, Vivienne mounted her soapbox in front of a baffled audience. She proclaimed: "The human race is going down the tube" and children were like "seeds with no nourishment". She advised that everyone should "Throw away your TVs as soon as possible" because "The best accessory you can give your children is a book" and "The key words are discrimination and elegance, and that's what a consumer should remember when buying. Schiaparelli said it best: 'Buy expensive or buy cheap'."[127]

In 1990, she was in the running to become Designer-in-Chief for the house of Sir Norman Hartnell, but lost out to Marc

Bohan, who was considered a more viable financial choice. She had also been disappointed by the failure of Pagan V, but her next collection, Portrait, for Autumn/Winter 1990, would mark a huge turning point in her career. It was the start of a new design era that recreated the lavish sexuality of eighteenth-century paintings, with the corsets, the pearls, the fake furs, and the portraits printed onto fabric as fashion and art fused together.

Vivienne's creativity was sparked by her visits to the Wallace Collection at Hertford House in Manchester Square, London, where she delved into the works of eighteenth-century French artists Jean-Antoine Watteau, François Boucher and Jean-Honoré Fragonard. She absorbed the Watteau dresses, the Georgian riding coats and corsets; the lushness of the folds of luxurious velvet, lace and tartans, and the drop pearl earrings to represent wealth and purity. She didn't just want to mimic the style, she wanted these paintings to be visually central to it. Boucher's

ABOVE LEFT Vivienne outside her Davies Street shop, holding her 1990 Fashion Designer of the Year award.

OPPOSITE Naomi Campbell in a rose print peignoir for the Spring/Summer 1993 Grand Hotel collection.

RIGHT Sara Stockbridge carrying her baby on the catwalk during the Cut, Slash and Pull Spring/Summer 1991 show.

OPPOSITE Vivienne with Susie Bick and Sara Stockbridge during London Fashion Week, March 1992.

Shepherd Watching a Sleeping Shepherdess was printed onto the "Stature of Liberty" corsets, the fabric designs of the antique furniture were replicated on stretch velvet, and she wove a tweed in the colours that matched the landscapes of Gainsborough.[128]

There were stretchy black velvet dresses and bodysuits embossed with gold foil rococo, a close-fit jacket with a huge sheepskin collar, as if a sheep was slung over the shoulders, earrings with drop pearls, Stewart tartan jackets, pinstripe suits worn with Boucher-printed ties, and the elevated platform shoes "to put my lady on a pedestal: I wanted her to look as though she'd just stepped out of a painting." For this collection she also created a "Dangerous Liaisons" jacket, named for both the 1782 novel and the 1988 film, and like the costumes in the movie, the corsets pushed up and exposed the breasts.

"[CUT AND SLASH] ENRICHES THE SURFACE AND GIVES CLOTHES A GALLANT, SWASHBUCKLING LOOK BY BRINGING MOVEMENT AND LIFE TO THEM."

Portrait was heralded in British *Vogue,* and not only did the coverage boost sales, but in October 1990 she was finally named British Designer of the Year. She won the prestigious title

"IT'S VERY DIFFICULT TO FIND A STUDENT WHO YOU'D GIVE A 100 OUT OF A 100 ... BUT IN THE CASE OF ANDREAS, HE WAS COMPLETELY OFF THE SCALE."

again in October 1991, with Sir Ralph Halpern, Chairman of the British Fashion Council, praising her as "an example of Britain at its most creative. The award was a mark of respect for her talents. She has influenced the fashion scene for a long time. She deserves it."[129]

In July 1990, she was invited to be a guest designer for an Italian gala evening in the Villa Gamberaia in Tuscany, where she designed her first menswear collection, Cut and Slash. It was an experimentation of shredded shirts and denims, inspired by a renaissance trend where luxurious fabric was pulled through slashes in outer garments, as a means of showing off riches. She said this approach "enriches the surface and gives clothes a gallant, swashbuckling look by bringing movement and life to them", and alongside the pirate-like slashes, she brought in codpieces.[130] The only female model in the show was Susie Bick in a slashed circle dress, and with its folds of fabric, it was designed to resemble Jan van Eyck's *The Arnolfini Portrait*.[131]

She followed it with Cut, Slash and Pull for Spring/Summer 1991, which took pieces from the previous menswear show, such as the ripped and slashed denims and pink satins, and printed rose fabric, and played with gender fluidity by putting the codpieces on women. As with Portrait, there were Boucher portraits printed onto swimsuits, and in one of her surreal touches, fabric was printed with close-up photography of human hair. It was feminine and flirty, and at the close of the show, Sara Stockbridge came out onto the catwalk as a bride carrying her newborn son, and wearing a gown printed with Fragonard's *The Swarm of Cupids*.

Women's Wear Daily praised Vivienne for being one of the few designers at London Fashion Week in October 1990 to come up with new ideas, offering a romantic femininity in a town "drowning in cotton and Lycra spandex". The collection was "so nostalgic that she topped her snap-on phallic symbols with roses and bows", and the "other ideas of her collection were long, unstructured Louise Brooks-style suits and slashed clothing she says is drawn from a fashion craze in the 15th century."[132]

Browns, the designer store on London's South Molton Street, stocked their first Vivienne Westwood pieces from the Cut, Slash and Pull collection, devoting two window displays to her.[133] The question was why it had taken so long, and Jean Bennett,

ABOVE A red rayon satin jacket from the Cut, Slash and Pull collection for Spring/Summer 1991.

ABOVE Vivienne with husband Andreas Kronthaler, working on the Spring/Summer 1992 Salon show.

Vivienne's press officer at the time, blamed the British press, "who can't seem to do enough to strangle their home-grown talents. They have traditionally been slow to applaud their own stars but are like lightning when it comes to devoting whole pages to Versace and Gaultier."[134]

While it was the outrageous fig leaf tights and codpieces that made headlines, they often overlooked the expert tailoring using fine tweeds and wools. Liz Tilberis, editor-in-chief of British *Vogue*, was a self-confessed fan. "Her last three collections have just been wonderful, she has been getting better and better."[135]

Assisting her on the Cut, Slash and Pull collection was a young Austrian designer, Andreas Kronthaler, who would become the next important man in her life. In 1988, as she struggled with finances, she accepted a teaching role, succeeding Karl Lagerfeld as Professor of Fashion at the Vienna Academy of Applied Arts, where she was paid £4,000 for working three days a month. She was wounded when she heard that a teaching colleague had cautioned her students that Vivienne wasn't a "real designer",[136] but over the course of her 13 years in the post, she used her teacher training and self-taught dressmaking skills to hammer the importance of technique to her students. In her first year of teaching, Andreas, a blacksmith's son from Tyrol, Austria, was quick to set himself apart as her top student with an eye for detail, and an appreciation of the technicalities behind couture.

"It's very difficult to find a student who you'd give a 100 out of a 100 – maybe it's possible, but I haven't met them yet," she later said. "But in the case of Andreas, he was completely off the scale."[137] They went on a date together to see the Old Master paintings at the Kunsthistorisches Museum, and he recalled that she "looked a sensation. She wore a chocolate brown stretch-velvet catsuit. A scarf draped around her hip. Her rocking-horse shoes. A leopard fake fur in pink. And her curls, in orange." It was in that moment, he would later remember, that he knew he wanted to be with her.[138] He was 25 years younger than her, but there were secret glances in the classroom and a mutual affection growing. When he created a collection of gowns inspired by the Renaissance, Vivienne was so impressed that she invited him to develop them in London, and after assisting her on Portrait, he stayed by her side as her collaborator and boyfriend. With issues around his right to work given he was from Austria, a non-EU country at the time, she and Andreas married secretly at Wandsworth Register Office in south London on 14 May 1992, with the news not reaching the press until over a year later. "It's a funny thing, because he was my boyfriend and I was saying to him, 'We have to find someone for you to marry, and then it'll be all right.' And he said, 'Well, I should marry you,'" she later recounted.[139] There was a cosiness to their relationship, as they cycled together to her studio every day, and he became more and more involved in the directions of her collections.

In March 1991, Azzedine Alaïa invited Vivienne to show her Autumn/Winter collection in his Paris showroom free of charge. He was a great admirer of her work and believed that her status meant that she should be doing her catwalk in Paris, but with her financial struggles she'd been unable to for the last six years. Dressing Up was elegant tailoring from the eighteenth century, and was an extravagant contrast to the age of grunge and the minimalist fashions of Calvin Klein.

The showroom was packed with designers and celebrities, including Christian Lacroix, Jean Paul Gaultier, Betty Jackson and John Galliano, as she showed some of her previous hits, including Harris tweed, red barathea wool hunting jackets, the ornate eighteenth-century decoration of Charles Boulle printed onto stretchy dresses and corsets, skirts with leather codpieces, "Love" jackets with heart-shaped lapels, and leopard print studded with satin bows. Vivienne wanted to reverse the trend for underdressing, where T-shirts and jeans had become a ubiquitous

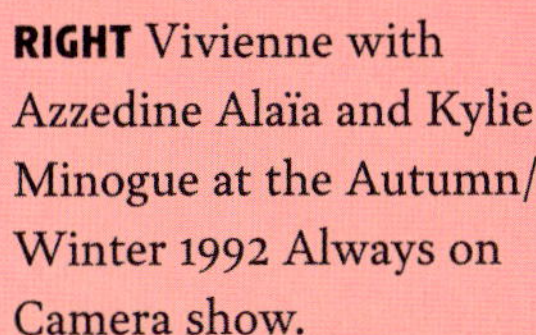

RIGHT Vivienne with Azzedine Alaïa and Kylie Minogue at the Autumn/Winter 1992 Always on Camera show.

uniform, and instead promoted elegance with her corsets, mini-crinis and platform shoes, which together manipulated a new posture and new silhouette. It proved to be a huge success as orders arrived from stores across Europe and the United States. She was about to turn 50, and she was finally in control and self-financed. She now had a shop, Vivienne Westwood, on Davies Street, Mayfair, and thanks to its prestigious location, it was attracting high-profile customers.

Vivienne had been one of the first designers to use diverse models on her catwalk, choosing older and more curvaceous women, such as Birgit, a grey-haired college administrator in her fifties from Vienna, Bertie Hope-Davies, a country gent in his sixties, and Jibby Beane, who was a similar age to Vivienne and worked in her store. In March 1990, a pregnant Sara Stockbridge strutted down the catwalk in a skin-tight velvet unitard, at a time when expectant mothers were supposed to hide their bodies. And then, later in the show, she was topless under a red fur-trimmed coat. While Pat Cleveland had been a very pregnant Virgin Mary in Thierry Mugler's 1984 show, London fashion hadn't seen anything like it.

Vivienne had enjoyed seeing her curvaceous pin-up girl models drunkenly stumble down the catwalk, but Andreas suggested to her that by using supermodels, she would be guaranteed coverage. Linda Evangelista had famously declared that she wouldn't get out of bed for less than $10,000 and so Vivienne knew she would never be able to afford their fees. But given her provocative reputation, supermodels like Linda and Naomi Campbell, then later Kate Moss, were willing to work for her in exchange for clothing. Her shows were always fun, and she encouraged them to show their personality rather than being a blank slate.

The Spring/Summer 1992 Salon collection, also shown in Alaïa's showroom, took the notion of the intellectual salon of writers and artists as she played with gender fluidity, and it

earned her not only her best reception in the UK and in Asia, but relaunched her as a designer of technique and artistic prestige. Naomi Campbell took to the catwalk alongside Sara Stockbridge, and they played as artists in berets and paint-splattered smocks, and then for the finale were dressed in contrasting black and white tulle gowns.

Given the press that Vivienne was now attracting, and the British Designer of the Year clout, she signed a deal in 1992 with the high street brand SockShop, where she printed a Boulle design onto sheer bodies and leggings. There was also a deal with Swatch for a limited-edition Orb watch. This all helped her solvency, and she was able to move into a larger studio in former school buildings in Battersea. There were also three labels introduced – Gold Label, which was the expensive couture; ready-to-wear Red Label, which offered more affordable pieces to help fund the Gold label; and a Blue Label for denim.

By the time she showed her Always on Camera collection for Autumn/Winter 1992, which paid tribute to Marlene Dietrich and Hollywood costume of the 1930s, fights broke out at Le Monde de l'Art in Paris in March 1992 as fans struggled to gain entry. Coming just a year after Madonna released 'Vogue', Vivienne's take on Hollywood glamour was a response to the sportswear and grunge movement. One of the focal points was a blow-up image from the '30s of Dietrich in a man's suit, which

ABOVE LEFT Leopard print and love hearts for the Always on Camera collection for Autumn/Winter 1992.

ABOVE Showing Marlene Dietrich denim, from the Always on Camera collection.

OPPOSITE Love heart sheer knickers, as part of the Always on Camera collection.

was then printed onto denim, and cut to form different parts of a garment, such as "eyes on the bum pocket, lips on the crotch", as Andreas Kronthaler later told *W* magazine.[140]

In tribute to Dietrich's fondness for androgyny, there were oversized men's suits in Scottish estate tweed, but also a pink leopard-print design, like shocking pink kisses, which would become a signature fabric pattern. Vivienne explained after the show that she "wanted to move into 20th century couture, and when I looked at it I realized Hollywood was the place where all that happened."[141]

Thanks to the movie star glamour of You're Always on Camera, *Women's Wear Daily* named Vivienne as one of the standouts at London Fashion Week in March 1992 alongside Jean Muir. "Westwood brought movie star glam to jeans, cutting them straight-legged, high waisted and with side buttons," said the review. "Despite the distractions of such accessories as fake moustaches and sideburns, banana skins and werewolf teeth, the higher standard came shining through."[142]

Grand Hotel for Spring/Summer 1993 similarly echoed old-time glamour, with its name taken from the 1932 Greta Garbo movie, and for the venue where it was shown – Paris's Grand Hotel. She played with the idea of the comings

ABOVE Tizer Bailey in a corset from the Portait collection at Clothes Show Live, NEC, Birmingham in December 1990.

"WESTWOOD BROUGHT MOVIE STAR GLAM TO JEANS, CUTTING THEM STRAIGHT-LEGGED, HIGH WAISTED AND WITH SIDE BUTTONS."

Women's Wear Daily

RIGHT The Grand Hotel Spring/Summer 1993 collection during Paris Fashion Week, October 1992.

and goings of a hotel lobby on the Riviera, with gowns and robes, bikinis, gold lurex, sunglasses and sun motifs, and with Sara Stockbridge in a yachting cap, shorts and pirate shirt, clutching a bottle of champagne. There was also a tribute to '50s tailoring with the "Bettina" jacket, named after the '50s Dior model Bettina Graziani.

By the time of Anglomania in 1993, such was her pull that all the top supermodels, Christy Turlington, Naomi Campbell and Linda Evangelista, walked down the catwalk with fledging stars Kate Moss, Eva Herzigova and Nadja Auermann. There was a huge demand to get hold of tickets for the show, held in Paris's Les Salons du Cercle Republicain. The collection took its name from the period just before the French Revolution when Paris swapped frock coats and wigs for an English style inspired by classical Greece. As well as the fine tailoring, of riding jackets and capes and trouser-suits, it was also heavy with tartan, as mini-kilts and plaids were worn with argyle-print tights and feathered bonnets. She commissioned Lochcarron of Scotland to design her

ABOVE Vivienne with her muse, model Sara Stockbridge (l), at a showing of the Portrait collection at Tall Orders in Soho, London, 1991.

OPPOSITE Anglomania Autumn/Winter 1993 Ready-to-Wear show.

own MacAndreas tartan, in tribute to Andreas. For the show's finale, Kate Moss emerged in a voluminous MacAndreas tartan wedding gown and veil.

There was one moment in the show that would guarantee the collection hit the headlines the next day – Naomi Campbell tumbling on the catwalk in her sky-high platforms. When Naomi interviewed Vivienne Westwood for a *Vogue* magazine video in 2019, she reflected on the moment. "I was embarrassed," she said. "I felt like I should have practiced more ... the most important thing is that I said to myself get up and keep going, that's all you have to do." Vivienne reassured her that it was the rubber tights that had knocked her off balance, and when she came back on the catwalk she was given a walking stick to hold on to in case she tripped again. Naomi also confessed that other designers asked her if she would fall on purpose for them, given the amount of publicity Vivienne had received for the tumble.

By this time, Vivienne's designs had shaped the mood of Paris's ready-to-wear collection. The corset was an essential for evening wear, while mini-crinolines and bell-shaped skirts were a common silhouette, and her tights and leggings worn with fitted jackets was reinterpreted by other designers as a cutting edge new look. Vivienne had shaken the standards of modern fashion, shifting it to one of decadence in the face of grunge and sportswear. Yet she always wanted to innovate and to push boundaries, because everything in her mind, she said, "starts from an intellectual point".

PLATFORM SHOES

When Naomi Campbell lost her balance while parading Vivienne's sky-high platforms on the Paris catwalk in March 1993, her legs sliding under her like a giraffe's, this dramatic tumble hit the headlines around the world. It was one of those unforgettable moments, alongside Kate Moss topless and eating a Magnum, that defined the Westwood catwalk shows in the 1990s.

The Super Elevated Gillie Platforms, in blue mock-crocodile, were part of the Anglomania collection for Autumn/Winter 1993, and featured ribbon laces which harked back to the eighteenth century. With a 12-inch (30.5 centimetre) heel, they proved a challenge for even the most skilled catwalk model. The incident helped to elevate the status of Westwood's platform heels. Rather than fretting about the optics of the incident, Westwood was thrilled. She later said the fall was "spectacular. It was better than an animal that's just being killed."

Vivienne had been experimenting with the architecture of eccentric footwear from her early design years at the King's Road shop. Creations included her 1974 SEX stilettos, and then the rocking horse platforms first revealed in the 1985 Mini-Crini collection. These were originally designed to help with posture and poise, and were inspired by *okobo*, the traditional wooden clogs worn by Japanese geisha.

Historically, platforms were added to the sole of the shoe as a support, but Vivienne covered the entire shoe and platform with leather or fabric, which, she said, "is a simple thing but makes them radically more beautiful: an extension of the whole look, and the leg." She created them in a range of textiles and colours, including in gingham fabric, tartan, leather and mock croc. The Super Elevated Gillies were an extreme form of platform shoe, sexual and evoking bondage, as they brought power and status to the wearer. By having them so high, so bulky, they were "a bit kinky", but without the extreme arch in the foot which made it difficult to stand all day. In this way, she saw them as both a feminine and feminist form of footwear.

As Westwood explained to fashion journalist Suzy Menkes in *The New York Times* in 1993: "I did the shoes for practical reasons, because you can't wear shoes all day if they have got a high angle. But when I did the platform with a heel, I was also saying that I wanted to put women on a pedestal. You feel so much more feminine and the center of attention. And when it comes to young people, they like the idea of being big."

She was even spotted about London with her hair in her distinctive red curls as she pedalled her bicycle in her elevated platform shoes. "Women should be on pedestals," she said. "Like art ... Or look like they have stepped out of a portrait. I wear them all the time."

RIGHT Naomi Campbell trips on the catwalk at the Vivienne Westwood Anglomania Autumn/Winter 1993 Ready-to-Wear show.

RIGHT The Super Elevated Ghillie boots, worn by Naomi Campbell when she famously tripped.

OPPOSITE A pair of Vivienne Westwood Super Elevated Lace-up ankle boots from 1993 are displayed prior to "Vivienne Westwood Shoes: An Exhibition 1973–2010" at Selfridges Ultra Lounge in London, 25 August 2010.

7

FASHION PROVOCATEUR

OPPOSITE Vivienne attends the opening of the "Court Couture '92" exhibition at Kensington Palace in London, July 1992.

BELOW Vivienne giving a revealing twirl to photographers at Buckingham Palace after receiving the OBE from Queen Elizabeth II in 1992.

In an interview with *Women's Wear Daily* in November 1992, Vivienne was reminded of an experimental necklace that Andreas Kronthaler had made using raw cubes of meat. "It looked really good when it went greenish," she said.[143] As demonstrated by this idea, two decades before Lady Gaga wore a meat dress to the MTV Video Music Awards, Vivienne was continually considering innovations and shock tactics.

By the 1990s, Vivienne was well aware that an outrageous moment had the power to garner huge amounts of publicity. In June 1992, she was invited to Kensington Palace for an event hosted by Princess Michael of Kent to launch the exhibition "Court Couture '92", a contemporary interpretation of royal dress. She made an elegant entrance in one of her black lace dresses with the delicate eighteenth-century Boulle design, but having opted to go without underwear, she realized too late that it was now translucent under the camera lights.

In December 1992, she experienced another wardrobe malfunction, this time at Buckingham Palace, after being presented with her OBE from the Queen. Outside the palace, photographers encouraged her to twirl in her Dior-inspired flannel suit and circle skirt, but forgetting she wasn't wearing underwear, she gave them a flash of more than they were expecting. "I hadn't decided on purpose not to wear knickers. In fact, I hardly ever wear knickers; I find them constricting," she said.[144] She later heard from someone at the palace that rather than being shocked, the Queen had found it hilarious.

Vivienne was now treated as one of Britain's great eccentrics, nicknamed "Viv" in the tabloids, and with her appearances at events guaranteed to bring fun and drama. Kate Moss adored her,

"THERE'S REAL ANARCHY IN THOSE GARMENTS ... NO, YOU'D BETTER NOT SAY ANARCHY. PEOPLE GET NERVOUS WHEN THEY HEAR THAT WORD."

later revealing to British *Vogue* that with her first big paycheck she splurged on a Vivienne Westwood coat ("sheepskin and it was pale blue to the floor. So beautiful. I still have it").

At the British Designer of the Year Awards, held in October 1993 at the Natural History Museum, Vivienne was surrounded by her devoted supermodels Kate and Naomi, who walked her catwalk in exchange for clothing rather than for a fee. Naomi, dressed in an Anglomania tartan suit and high platform heels – the same ones she had taken a tumble in – playfully ran into Vivienne's arms to pose for photos. "Naomi Campbell got quite carried away," ran the *Daily Mirror* the next day. As she stretched into the splits, "the larger-than-life designer Vivienne Westwood hoisted her in her arms."[145]

By the time Vivienne brought Café Society (Spring/Summer 1994) to Paris Fashion Week in October 1993, she was the top attraction because her shows were all but guaranteed to have attention-grabbing happenings that would be gossiped about for days. The show, held at the Grand Hotel, Paris, mixed the high drama of the historical references in her designs with

RIGHT With Naomi Campbell at the Designer of the Year Awards at the Natural History Museum during London Fashion Week, October 1993.

OPPOSITE Vivienne with models at the Café Society Spring/Summer 1994 show in Paris.

publicity-grabbing spectacle. There was something deliciously decadent about Kate Moss making her way down the leopardskin carpet of the catwalk, parading topless while licking a Magnum ice cream.

The collection was an homage to the first French couturier, Charles Worth, while exploring the idea of the nineteenth-century salon as a licentious, intellectual space where the upper echelons always dressed well. "There's real anarchy in those garments," Vivienne said of Worth. "No, you'd better not say anarchy. People get nervous when they hear that word. They think it means chaos."[146] As well as Kate, topless and wearing the tiniest striped skirt, a pirate hat on her head and the orb necklace draped down her chest, the other supermodels resembled portraits of Queen Elizabeth I, as if she were transplanted to the Riviera of 1900, with the slender jackets and long narrow skirts.

Their hair was curled and piled on top of their heads to mimic Elizabethan styles, their faces heavily powdered and accentuated with berry lips and beauty spots, and there were eighteenth-century French frock coats, knitted tassels like those of Charles Worth, rustling baroque gowns, striped blazers and napkin hats, and pencil skirts worn with misbuttoned cardigans. As she had done with her mini-crini, Vivienne was playing with, and asking the question of, what unrestricted freedom for women looked like, and used all her historical reference points to challenge the status quo.

"THAT COLLECTION WAS SO BEAUTIFUL, I FEEL REALLY LUCKY TO HAVE HAD THAT EXPERIENCE."

Kate Moss

ABOVE Carla Bruni wears the fur G-string for the On Liberty Autumn/Winter 1994 show at Paris Fashion Week, March 1994.

OPPOSITE Kate Moss eating a Magnum ice-cream during the Café Society show, at Paris Fashion Week in October 1993.

For Kate Moss, it was one of the most memorable of her catwalk moments. "This was one of my favourites," she told British *Vogue* in 2022, as she looked back at photos from her career. "It was a Magnum ice cream and they just said, 'Eat that as you go out with no top on.' And I was like, 'Yeah I'll try.' I managed that. And those heels as well. That skirt, I've got one and Lila [her daughter] she's like, 'Mummy! It's so short!' Yeah, you're supposed to see your knickers. That collection was so beautiful, I feel really lucky to have had that experience."

As a reaction to the androgyny of sportswear, Vivienne enjoyed enhancing women's bodies by pushing up the breasts with her corsets, and extending the legs with the platform shoes that forced a change of posture for the wearer. Now, in her next collection she played with the hips and posterior to reset the modern silhouette.

On Liberty (Autumn/Winter 1994) was inspired by the English philosopher John Stuart Mill and his call for individual freedom, as she idealized the female form by amplifying the nineteenth-century bustle with padding on the buttocks, to contrast with exaggerated shoulders and nipped-in waists. This was her first collaboration with Liberty, where her knitted dresses and fabric prints were drawn from the Liberty archives, but all the press attention focused on these "unwearable" bustles. There were also other "viral" moments from the show. Kate Moss pulled her black corset down to expose her breasts, and at a time when she was chastised for being too thin, this led to accusations of child pornography, despite Kate being an adult. One of the most mesmerizing moments, and which received whoops from the crowd, was when Carla Bruni strutted down the catwalk in a faux fur coat and red heels, only to open it and reveal she was wearing a G-string with a fur patch, like a merkin.

In September 1994, Vivienne arrived in New York to bring her fashion show to Bergdorf Goodman department store, where the room was staged like a theatrical dinner, as if from the film *Barry Lyndon*. Tables were set with flower arrangements and silver centrepieces filled with sugared nuts, candy and fresh fruits, and Vivienne sat next to Bergdorf's president Dawn Mello, as fashion editors and photographers buzzed around. "If you look

ABOVE Vivienne created bum cages to enhance the silhouette for the On Liberty collection.

LEFT Argyle knit bodysuits and sweaters in the On Liberty Autumn/Winter 1994 show.

OPPOSITE Linda Evangelista wearing the Bruce of Kinnaird tartan skirt, shirt and tie, with plaid, sporran and tam, on the Anglomania catwalk.

"WHEN YOU WEAR MY CLOTHES YOU WILL BE NOTICED. THE CLOTHES HAVE A RAPPORT WITH THE BODY."

at the clothes, the detail is extraordinary," said Mello. "This is the first season we've had her, but I've always admired her direction. She's maybe the most important fashion leader we have today."[147]

The models were sent down the catwalk wearing some of Vivienne's greatest hits, including platform stilettos with equestrian jackets and bum-padded crocheted dresses, the "Bettina" jacket, the grey "Dangerous Liaisons" jacket with red fur trim, and what Vivienne had dubbed the "Masturbation skirt", for its fabric pushed up at the front. Closing the show was the larger-than-life Dianne Brill, an It girl of the downtown club scene in the 1980s who was named "Queen of the Night" by Andy Warhol. "The clothes are very strong," Vivienne told a reporter from *Women's Wear Daily*. "Not everybody can wear them. When you wear my clothes you will be noticed. The clothes have a rapport with the body. These clothes are really quite tight. You think it's the wrong size at first."[148]

By 1994, Vivienne's fortunes had turned around and she had a turnover of £3 million, which grew to £20 million by 1998. Profits were bolstered by her newfound popularity in the more conservative United States, with Bergdorf Goodman having ordered pieces from the On Liberty collection, and Saks Fifth Avenue following in 1995. There were three shops in London, with plans to expand to Paris, and as well as her Gold Label (manufactured in London) and Red Label (manufactured in bigger quantities in Italy to keep the prices down), she wanted to go more "toward made-to measure", with the bridal gowns and debutante-style evening wear.[149]

In 1993, she struck a deal with Brintons, a carpet manufacturer based in Kidderminster, in which Vivienne designed gowns made from their heavy carpets. These were then draped on models and photographed by David Bailey. She and Brintons teamed up again in 1999 for another campaign in which the carpets were styled into eighteenth-century gowns, with the tagline "classic carpet since 1783".

She continued to capitalize on her popularity when she accepted an invitation by Littlewoods to design for their home shopping catalogue. This collection of affordable pieces, boasting the orb logo, was launched in 1993 and modelled by Cheshire-born Susie Bick, who, in the '90s was one of the most important of Vivienne's muses.

OPPOSITE The Axminster carpet dress, from a collection designed by Vivienne for a Brinton's carpet advertising campaign. The dress weighs 33 lb (15 kg) and the back of the carpet was softened to manipulate it into shape.

ABOVE Naomi Campbell wearing a siren for a hat, during the On Liberty catwalk show.

Vivienne was inspired to do a high street collaboration when she was being driven to the opening of a club one night, and saw the police barricades keeping back the crowds. As the cars queued up outside the venue, Vivienne was spotted by a group of girls who started chatting to her. "They said they really liked my clothes but there was no way they could ever afford them," she said. "Then they asked why I never designed anything for people with very little money."

The Littlewoods deal was an opportunity to provide clothes for those on a budget, particularly since she had been so scathing about what was currently available on the high street. "The whole world is becoming more crude, more garish," she complained. "I blame the Americans – and, particularly, Hollywood. I call it Wallyhood. It's responsible for so much mediocrity ... I wouldn't outlaw denim altogether because it's such a nice fabric and you can do so much with it. But trainers! Whenever I see someone wearing them, a little bell goes off in my mind ... Brain damage."[150]

In an interview in 1993, she suggested that Princess Diana could boost her fashion credentials by choosing pieces from the mail-order catalogue. She criticized Diana's choice of power suits with shoulder pads, and the "horrible little pumps that are neither one thing or the other". She said she wasn't suggesting Diana wear her Littlewoods pieces for public appearances because they'd be "too provocative", but for her private wardrobe, "Why not?"[151]

It was these bold statements that helped to make her such a tabloid favourite in the UK, and made her ripe for send-up in Robert Altman's satire of the fashion world, *Prêt-à-Porter* (1994), set during Paris Fashion Week. Richard E. Grant played the male equivalent of Vivienne with his eccentric catwalk moments, including placing a traffic siren on one model's head, as Vivienne had done to Naomi Campbell. Never taking herself too seriously, Vivienne was one of the few designers who agreed to make a cameo, and Susie Bick also played herself backstage at Vivienne's show, and took part in the naked catwalk in the movie's finale.[152]

ABOVE Westwood arriving at the Naomi Campbell book launch, Charing Cross Road, London, 5 September 1994.

LEFT Vivienne and her son, Joe Corré, on his Agent Provocateur opening night, 1994.

LEFT Vivienne and her Husband Andreas Kronthaler at Royal Ascot, 20 June 1995.

OPPOSITE Vivienne backstage during Paris Fashion Week in March 1995, wearing the knitted floral top from the On Liberty collection.

Vivienne's continued popularity during Paris Fashion Week was evident in October 1994 at the Erotic Zones collection for Spring/Summer 1995, where prestigious front row seats were taken by Lenny Kravitz, Kylie Minogue and Vanessa Paradis. The extreme, ultra feminine silhouettes were enhanced by the "Cul cage", a lightweight wire bustle that was tied to a girdle with ribbons, and which had been created by Andreas Kronthaler's blacksmith father.

"All the great male designers like Saint Laurent, like Dior, they make women look like goddesses," she said. "I want to dress them to look important. Like a hero." Her focus was on those areas of the body that she felt that the current trends, for grunge and waifish models, had forgotten. These exaggerated buttocks, and the gingham fabrics of blouses and gloves, would be borrowed by Comme des Garçons' "lumps and bumps" collection for Spring/Summer 1997. "The atmosphere is pure theatre," Susie Bick was quoted as saying. "This season Vivienne asked us to be very grand and puffed up with Edwardian pride."

Her next shows, for Autumn/Winter 1995, and Spring/Summer 1996, named Vive la Cocotte and Les Femmes, were an eighteenth-century feast of French court fashions. The names

"ALL THE GREAT MALE DESIGNERS LIKE SAINT LAURENT, LIKE DIOR, THEY MAKE WOMEN LOOK LIKE GODDESSES ... I WANT TO DRESS THEM TO LOOK IMPORTANT. LIKE A HERO."

RIGHT Model Nadja Auermann at the Les Femmes Ne Connaissent Pas Toute Leur Coquetterie Spring/ Summer 1996 show.

OPPOSITE Printed corset dress from the same collection.

of the collections took inspiration from seventeenth-century authors Ninon de L'Enclos, whose text *La cocotte vengée* (The Flirt Avenged) called for enjoyment in life without religion, and François de La Rochefoucauld, whose statement "Les femmes ne connaissent pas toute leur coquetterie" translated as "Women don't know the full extent of their coquettishness."

For Vive la Cocotte, shown in March 1995, models with pale powdered faces and red lips, by make-up artist Mary Greenwell, boasted absolute hourglass figures through the 1950s bullet-bras of Vivienne's teenage memories, the "cul cage", or "bum cage", and high platform heels to manipulate their posture. It was the pinnacle of her desire to push the hourglass silhouette to extremes, and a reaction against what Vivienne described in the show notes as "the sloppy mediocrity of our age". The show was also a reflection of all that she loved, of the Highland Fling, *Dangerous Liaisons* and Madame de Pompadour, and the paganism of horns and fur.

Outside the venue, editors, fashion buyers and photographers jostled with students and fans to try to get past the security

"YOU'RE GOING TO SEE THE BEST LADIES DRESSED AS MEN YOU'VE SEEN IN A WHILE."

guards. Yet after struggling into the venue, a group of French reporters marched out of the show after waiting 40 minutes for it to start. They had collectively agreed to protest against the habit of designers delaying and dragging out the start of their shows, for which Vivienne was notorious. But as the lights dimmed, they must have regretted missing out on the spectacle. Linda Evangelista opened the show in a black tailored jacket, lined with sparkling glitter-ball fabric, and padded breasts, nipped-in waist and huge padded hips and butt transformed her into the idealized woman.

As the *Independent* wrote, "There was also a combination of clashing fabrics and what seemed like the entire BBC costume drama wardrobe: a Little Lord Fauntleroy suit with knickerbockers; a rose print bedspread skirt; a Queen of Sheba outfit with crystal and diamante bodice and feather skirt; and the Madam Pompadour gown."[153]

For those who weren't brave enough for the padding, Vivienne came up with the "Metropolitan" jacket. Encouraged by Andreas, she studied the New Look silhouette of Christian Dior, particularly a Dior jacket held at the Metropolitan Museum of Art, to create her own version with rounded shoulders, nipped-in waist and a lining of hair-print satin.

The Les Femmes show offered a less exaggerated silhouette of eighteenth-century femininity, this time with the bustles and padding removed, heels lowered, and with a slimmer silhouette. Rather than Madame de Pompadour, the inspiration was Marie Antoinette in her pastoral chemise dresses, making for a collection that was more wearable and therefore more commercial.

She admired the golden age of couture, and believed her strength was in the way she cut and treated the fabric. "I'm just trying to make things as good as people did in the past," she said in a 1994 interview with *Women's Wear Daily*. "A modern myth that should be demolished is that we live in an age where everything automatically becomes more modern, more comfortable and more futuristic. This is the only century that hasn't had respect for the past ... Where would I get ideas if they didn't come from the past? The great age of clothes was the couture until the 1950s. We have no hope unless we refer to the past."[154]

Her Autumn/Winter 1996 collection, Storm in a Teacup, shifted focus from the exaggerated padding to a more masculine

ABOVE Vivienne walks the runway at the finale of the Five Centuries Ago Autumn/Winter 1997 show.

ABOVE RIGHT Jerry Hall models for the Storm in a Teacup collection at Paris Fashion Week in March 1996.

silhouette. The influences included decorative rococo furniture, the unpredictable British weather, and the asymmetry of cut, which she described as "facing up to the horror of uniformity and minimalism". It was a concept she had played with since the Pirate collection, when she created a T-shirt with a neck hole in a different position, so that the fabric ruched.

While the storm of the title was because, she said, the "clothes are cut so they look like they're being blown", the teacup was for her emphasis on English tailoring. She combined British argyle knits with the special fabrics she developed with traditional men's tailors in London's Jermyn Street, which were mismatched with leopard print, tartan and stripes. "You're going to see the best ladies dressed as men you've seen in a while," she added.[155]

Vive la Bagatelle, for Spring/Summer 1997, was a celebration of the frivolous and the pretty, with "Bagatelle" meaning "nothing, a trifle", according to Vivienne. She credited husband Andreas for developing the silhouette, which featured bias-cut gowns, ripened fruit prints, and camouflage bras worn over shirts, first seen in Nostalgia of Mud. Harking back to her bondage collection at SEX were restrictive S&M sleeves, as if "her body is being held back."[156]

Five Centuries Ago, for Autumn/Winter 1997, drew inspiration from the Hans Holbein Tudor and Jacobean portraits which were displayed at the Tate London exhibition "Dynasties" in 1995. The Elizabethan designs featured standing collars, rich brocade coats, Watteau jackets and corsets with flashes of breasts, skirts that were gathered up to expose suspenders, and zipped leather suits. In tribute to the Jacobites, a piper led the models in a procession of tartan confections. Alek Wek closed the show wearing a farthingale gown of silk printed with land and sea beasts, which was directly inspired by a portrait of Queen Elizabeth I displayed at Hardwick Hall, Derbyshire.

This time, rather than platitudes, *Women's Wear Daily* was critical of Vivienne's work, lamenting that "the bloom has definitely faded from Westwood's historical indulgences. And that's a shame." The reporter described her as "a great talent and a superior technician. Her sense of fabric and color is remarkable, as is the intricacy of her cuts ... But there is a fine line between iconoclasm and arrogance ... Perhaps, as we stand on the brink of the 21st century, Westwood should consider entering the 20th."[157]

The Holbein portraits would also inspire her first major advertising campaign, a move deemed necessary given that the glossy magazines skewed their editorial towards the fashion houses who took out expensive advertising space. She commissioned illustrator Richard Gray to create drawings based on the portraits, and then photographer Gian Paolo Barbieri interpreted them to depict Vivienne as Elizabeth I, Andreas as Robert Devereux, Second Earl of Essex, and with Jerry Hall also in regal attire.

Vivienne's brand was going from strength to strength as part of a strategy to take her from cult favourite to mainstream designer. After Red Label was launched in 1993, Vivienne Westwood Man was first shown in January 1996 in Milan, and then in 1997 she introduced Anglomania, manufactured under the GTR Group of Italy. This new line was designed for a younger, edgier customer who wanted to buy into the rebellious, romantic spirit for less.

In June 1998, she launched her signature scent, Boudoir. Developed by Lancaster under a licensing deal, it was sold exclusively at Harvey Nichols before being rolled out across Europe. "It was very stressful doing a perfume because it's so intangible," she said. "But I felt it was important to complete the capsule of my business."[158]

ABOVE From the Tied to the Mast collection for Spring/Summer 1998.

OPPOSITE Vivienne backstage during the La Belle Helene Spring/ Summer 1999 show at Paris Fashion Week, October 1998.

"I DON'T BELIEVE IN PROGRESS. FOR ME, IT'S A MATTER OF *NOT* KEEPING UP WITH THE TIMES."

OPPOSITE Alek Wek walking the runway for the Tied to the Mast Spring/Summer 1998 collection.

BELOW Wek wearing the reimagined Pirate rope print for the Tied to the Mast collection.

She wanted to add a sexier note to the classic fragrances she remembered from her youth, such as Schiaparelli's Shocking. While she conceived it as a tempting scent, she added, "What's most important is that it shouldn't repulse people and I don't think this does."[159]

Another ode to the Pirate collection was Tied to the Mast, for Spring/Summer 1998, where Théodore Géricault's paintings inspired a humorous fantasy of Elizabethan lady pirates shipwrecked on a desert island, forced to survive on the trunks that were washed up on shore. On the catwalk in the salon of Hotel de Crillon there were reimagined pirate boots, hats made from maps, sun-bleached denim, a variation of the rope print from Pirate, and windswept models with eyepatches, wearing jewellery that appeared as if it had been plundered. The finale featured Alek Wek in an imposing ballgown constructed from multicoloured distressed denim.[160]

Dressed to Scale, for Autumn/Winter 1998, was about "displacement and discombobulation", with inspiration coming from the folk costume of Andreas's childhood in Austria, and the satirical prints of Georgian England printmaker James Gillray, who used sartorial exaggeration in his caricatures. Vivienne had always been fascinated by playing with the size and scale of clothing, and there was an artificiality with oversized buttons on cropped jackets, skin-tight knit dresses, and a voluminous taupe taffeta gown.

Women's Wear Daily was once again critical of her obsession with the past, describing the half-skirts that revealed a model's derriere as "more comical than directional" and that the once influential designer now appeared to "have put her creative juices on hold".[161]

Despite the accusation that her historical references were becoming tired when other designers had their eye on the future, Vivienne Westwood would thrive in the millennium. She bit back, insisting that "I don't believe in progress. For me, it's a matter of *not* keeping up with the times."[162]

TARTAN

As Vivienne embraced British tradition and turned her eye to heritage fabrics, tartan was a consistent presence in many of her collections. Focusing on British tradition and tailoring, she thought of the political charge that is often woven through fabric, and tartan was in full dramatic glory in the Anglomania collection.

She appreciated the vibrancy of the different patterns of setts, and their symbolism – representing family belonging, military uniform, rebellion, nostalgia and national pride. Her use of tartan bridged the historical with the contemporary, adding new twists on one of the most traditional of textiles.

"The idea that there were particular tartans belonging to this house or another was developed by the Victorian tourist industry, but nevertheless it is traditional, these hand-woven clothes in stripes and check," said Vivienne. "It's a heroic image, the kilt flying and the idea of climbing mountains in this garb with the wind blowing behind you. They have all got stories, these fabrics."

Tartan was a vital component of the punk do-it-yourself look. Kilts could be bought from thrift stores and repurposed; they were held together by the safety pin, a punk staple, and tartan was also threaded with a sense of rebellion. As the Jacobites led the charge for Bonnie Prince Charlie, of the House of Stuart, to be reinstated on the British throne, the Royal Stuart tartan was the symbol of their cause. After their defeat at the Battle of Culloden, tartan was banned from being worn by Highlanders for 40 years. It was later revived by the British royal family, and in particular Queen Victoria, who imbued it with the romantic notion of the Highlander. The Stuart tartan, previously soaked in rebellion, became the official tartan of Queen Elizabeth II, who wore it when holidaying at Balmoral Castle. This chequered history was an appealing one for Vivienne, particularly when designing her bondage suits in 1977. She also appreciated the simplicity of the traditional Highland plaid, where a length of fabric was folded and pinned into a garment. She took the notion of the warriors of Culloden in their belted plaid and transformed them into "urban guerrillas".

The conflict between rebellion and establishment stayed with her. Tartan was incorporated into the Time Machine collection (Autumn/Winter 1988), where model Michael Clark, in full Highland dress, performed the sword dance, or the Ghillie Callum, to the sound of the bagpipes.

ABOVE Naomi Campbell in the Bruce of Kinnaird tartan for the Anglomania collection.

Tartan was also an important part of Anglomania (Autumn/Winter 1993) which was drawn from the late-eighteenth-century fad for British fashion in Paris, when the presence of Highland regiments in the city during the Napoleonic Wars had set a craze for women to wear tartan favours on their gowns. Her twist on this tradition was mixing French couture with British tailoring, swathes of clashing tartans, and tam o' shanter hats.

She even designed her own tartan for Anglomania, the MacAndreas, in honour of her husband, who she said was fascinated by the kilt and enjoyed promoting "robes and skirts for men". She worked with Lochcarron of Scotland, the world's leading manufacturer of tartan, to design and select the turquoise and copper dyes for this sett. She then added it to the official Scottish Register of Tartans. Vivienne enjoyed creating her own tartan so much that she continued to work with Lochcarron to develop new tartans for different collections, such as the purple and midnight blue MacPoiret, a tribute to French couturier Paul Poiret which was registered in 1993. MacBrick and MacStone, named for their colours, were registered in 1996, and Westwood MacSky was registered in 1997. She also returned to traditional weaves, from the classic Stuart tartan, so often seen on shortbread tins, to Bruce of Kinnaird, with its vibrant, green, pink and red, which she adopted for hand bags and gloves.

Given tartan's swagger, it was a vital component for the Vivienne Westwood Man label, with tartan trousers, kilts and bomber jackets all frequently shown.

For Spring/Summer 2023, Andreas further updated the MacAndreas tartan with neon yarns for tailored jackets, and draped, ruched dresses. Shown in October 2022, it would be the final collection before Vivienne's death that December, and so it was a fitting tribute to the woman considered such a lover, and a champion, of the Scottish textile industry.

ABOVE The On Liberty Autumn/Winter 1994 show, Paris, March 1994.

ABOVE Kate Moss models the McAndreas Tartan, at the Autumn/Winter 1993 show.

8

POLITICS VERSUS TRADITION

OPPOSITE Vivienne modelling her own designs from the Tied to the Mast collection, in her Soho office, 2004.

Partly down to the success of Anglomania, Vivienne's sales, by the turn of the millennium, were sitting at $42 million a year, and there were further plans to build on this.[163] In 2002, she conquered Asia by opening a boutique in Hong Kong, and two in South Korea, followed by the Japanese womenswear flagship boutique Aoyama in March 2003. She also teamed up with Comme des Garçons for an Autumn/Winter 2002 Vivienne Westwood X Commes des Garçons collection, which was launched in Japan and Milan. She was now one of the most recognizable global brands in Japan alongside Coca-Cola and Disney, thanks to the Japanese appreciation of British textiles and traditions.

Having turned 60 in April 2001, she was considered the grande dame of fashion, and with her pale face a contrast to her bouffant hair and scarlet lips, her age complemented her eccentricity. She was the "oldest ingénue in the fashion business"; she was "growing old disgracefully" and her Derbyshire accent was described by one interviewer as "sweet and gormless as a lollypop lady's".[164] She played up to and embraced her age. The final year collections for her students at Berlin's University of the Arts fashion department were modelled by the residents of an old people's home. "Life becomes richer as you grow old," she said. "I like the ageing process and have no problem with it."

"IF YOU WANT TO BE A FASHION DESIGNER, DON'T LOOK AT FASHION MAGAZINES. DON'T CARE ABOUT THEM. LOOK AT COSTUME."

She may have been a grandmother, but she was not willing to compromise. At a November 2000 picnic-style show in the gardens of the Sunset Marquis in West Hollywood she teamed a flouncing

LEFT Showcasing her Spring/Summer 2001 collection in the gardens of the Sunset Marquis hotel in West Hollywood, 14 November 2000.

OPPOSITE Vivienne cycling in London, September 2011.

purple skirt with a T-shirt which featured a pin-up flashing her buttocks. "I don't pretend like it's a crusade. But to offer choice in an age of conformity is a powerful thing," she said. "I could not go outside my house wearing anything from the Gap. I would feel like someone had taken my soul away."[165]

She and Andreas lived in bliss in an historic home in Clapham, dating from 1703. "One of my favorite 'rooms' is the garden, all overgrown, with a fantastic mimosa tree, a palm tree and 15 rose trees planted in pots," she said.[166] She credited her youthfulness to eating well and cycling to work, and she rejected plastic surgery. It was just one of the modern inventions she cursed, alongside computers, radio and television. And as she told her students, "If you want to be a fashion designer, don't look at fashion magazines. Don't care about them. Look at costume."

She professed her love of books, described it as her biggest passion in life and the source of her extensive historical references. Several pieces from her Spring/Summer 2001 collection,

ABOVE Vivienne Westwood Exploration collection for the Spring/ Summer 2001 show.

RIGHT The bookbinder print in the Exploration show was created from a photograph of Vivienne's bookshelves.

Exploration, featured a bookbinder print, where fabric had been printed with a close-up of the bookshelves in her home.[167]

Her home life was unconventional, and despite the age gap her marriage was a creative force of understanding, as they worked and lived seamlessly together. She and Andreas were so suited to each other "because we're both incredibly tolerant; it's beneath me to worry about being jealous of a man. He's got quite different friends than I have, lots of girlfriends; he loves beautiful women. If I have one vision of us working together, it's of him doing something incredibly grand, and me, the more mathematical one, developing all these cutting principles."[168]

As part of her Autumn/Winter 2001 collection, Wild Beauty, inspired by the drape of the garments on classical Greek statuary, she developed a new technique of allowing the fabric to be guided by the body. "I thought that a new way of getting that effect, but without the volume, would be to cut these curved seams. So I ended up with all these jigsaw puzzle shapes," she said. She described it as "spatial intelligence" and credited herself with "a real sense of three-dimensional geometry. I can look at a flat piece of fabric and know that if I put a slit in it and make

LEFT The revival of the Buffalo hat in the Exhibition collection for Autumn/Winter 2004.

OPPOSITE Vivienne's granddaughter, Cora, making her first catwalk appearance for the Wild Beauty collection Autumn/Winter 2001.

some fabric travel around a square, then when you lift it up it will drape in a certain way, and I can feel how that will happen."[169]

She had survived bankruptcy and ridicule, and been dismissed as humourless, despite continually revealing her prankish, satirical wit with her printed breasts on T-shirts for men, and her *Tatler* cover, when she was dressed as Thatcher. And now she was being revered by a new generation who admired the Pirate, Buffalo and Punkature collections, featured retrospectively in hip youth magazines *Dazed and Confused* and *i-D*.

Her impact was felt in the Autumn/Winter 2001 collections of Missoni, which borrowed the ethnic prints from the Pirate collection, and of Bottega Veneta, which borrowed the Keith Haring hieroglyphics, and just as she and Malcolm had pioneered bras over tops in 1982's Nostalgia of Mud, Comme des Garçons placed bras over deconstructed suits.[170]

> **"THEY'RE OBSESSED BY PRE-1984 VIVIENNE WESTWOOD ... BECAUSE IT'S THE COOLEST VINTAGE CRAZE AROUND."**
>
> Claudia Croft, *The Sunday Times*

ABOVE LEFT A model walks the runway for the Nymphs collection in October 2001, wearing a rugby jersey and skirt.

When Kate Moss was snapped in an original pair of Pirate boots in 2001, the surge in demand led to the boots being reissued, and original T-shirts from the 1970s were also being snapped up at auction. In 2008, Sotheby's listed a graphic T-shirt with two men having sex and the caption "Fuck your Mother ... Punk!"

As Claudia Croft wrote in her Planet Fashion column in *The Sunday Times* in April 2001, it was easy to spot a fashion junkie: "They're obsessed by pre-1984 Vivienne Westwood ... Because it's the coolest vintage craze around. The fashion director of *The Face*, Katie Grand, lives in her Buffalo collection sheepskin coat (autumn/winter 1982), Pirate collection boots (a/w 1981) and Witches collection printed scarf (a/w 1983). Kate Moss and Stella McCartney also have Pirate boots."[171]

With her past collections being lauded and emulated, Vivienne continued to reference her favourite historical influences. Nymphs, for Spring/Summer 2002, showed rococo pastoral scenes in the works of Fragonard, Boucher and Watteau. Models walked a woodland catwalk as if they were the nymphs of the title, with their long, long eyelashes, snail jewellery, lace dresses and hitched-up skirts, and they even wore rugby shirts, as had been alluded to in Civilizade.

RIGHT Vivienne with Kate Moss for the opening of the Vivienne Westwood retrospective exhibition at the Victoria and Albert Museum, London, 30 March 2004.

ABOVE Vivienne at press day for the opening of her retrospective exhibition held at the Victoria and Albert Museum.

To mark the Queen's Golden Jubilee in 2002, Vivienne's Anglophilia collection (Autumn/Winter 2002) had the historical swagger of past royal courts with a muted palette of tweeds and rich brocades, slashed double sleeves, lace-trimmed corsets, twinsets and a daring bubblegum-pink argyle knit bodysuit. It was a far cry from the 1977 Silver Jubilee, when she had outraged the establishment with a two-fingered salute to anarchy.

She did, however, return to street style and sportswear in Street Theatre for Spring/Summer 2003, where fashion was now a performance, as it had been in the days of punk. The first model entered the catwalk by breaking through the cordon tape of a construction site, and there were layers of shredded denim, oversized jackets with the belt strapped around the neckline, a voluminous coat tied with what looked like a garbage bag, and translucent ruffled, layered dresses.

In 2004, the Victoria and Albert Museum, as if capturing the hype, announced a retrospective exhibition to celebrate Vivienne's career so far. It opened in May, with 150 designs on display from the museum's collection and Vivienne's archive, all demonstrating the impact she had made in her 40 years as creator. Visitors were welcomed to the exhibition by the 13-hour,

"A PIN IS THE OLDEST WAY TO FASHION AND DECORATE CLOTHES."

LEFT Vivienne on the runway during her menswear show, Spring/ Summer 2005, Milan Fashion Week.

OPPOSITE Vivienne wearing the Propaganda dress from the collection of the same name, Autumn/Winter 2005.

backwards, Worlds End clock, as they were taken on a journey through all her innovations and provocations. At the opening night, admirers and celebrity friends were squeezed into corset tops, staggered in platform shoes or were wrapped in taffeta gowns to celebrate Vivienne's career. There was Kate Moss in an apple-green jersey dress from the Buffalo collection, Sam Taylor-Wood in a black silk corset and pleated denim miniskirt ("The best thing about Westwood's clothes? Breasts and bums," she said), Vivienne's catwalk muses Jerry Hall, Sadie Frost and Jibby Beane, as well as Sara Stockbridge in a black taffeta gown with roadkill stole. Vivienne arrived with husband Andreas and friend and latest muse Tracey Emin, wearing silver glitter horns, and a printed red silk gown from her latest collection.[172]

To coincide with this retrospective showcase, the Autumn/Winter 2004 collection was named Exhibition, and she looked back to her classics, such as the "Bettina", the bondage trousers in Stewart tartan, dresses restrained with straps, and the "Stature of Liberty" corset. Models walked on a catwalk with a backdrop of clothing rails and garments in protective bags, further paying tribute to her retrospective. The next collection, Ultra Femininity, for Spring/Summer 2005, harked back to the rococo influence of her 1990s collections, from the powdered complexions of her models to the corsets and straw hats, and classic draping. There were also elements from her Pirate collection, with the rope print on bags, and the chicken bones from the Let It Rock T-shirts now as a print.

In June 2005, she launched her first jewellery collection, Hardcore Diamonds, where the highlight, alongside some penis designs, was a white gold safety pin with a diamond dangle. "I love the safety pin for its humanity and functionality," she said. "A pin is the oldest way to fashion and decorate clothes."[173] She designed the collection in just a couple of hours, drawing on paper and making makeshift prototypes with safety pins, paper clips and tape from her worktable. She also featured the signature orb logo, covered in diamonds for cuff links and earrings.[174]

A year later, in May 2006, New York's Metropolitan Museum of Art Costume Institute held a new exhibition indebted to Vivienne's ideas of punk rebellion juxtaposed with aristocratic tradition. "AngloMania: Tradition and Transgression in British Fashion" showcased Vivienne's work alongside other modern

British designers, tailors and milliners including John Galliano, Alexander McQueen, Christopher Bailey for Burberry, and Stella McCartney. There were paintings by Gainsborough and Reynolds as a backdrop to the dresses, as if the eighteenth-century subjects had been dressed by Vivienne. The contemporary pieces stretched from 1976, to mark 30 years since the birth of punk, further demonstrating just how influential her work had been on other designers. But with punk now incorporated into the clean fabrics of fashion, the grimy anger and disaffection of its original wearers had been removed.

While she acknowledged that Christian Lacroix and John Galliano's brands had drawn from her own ideas, she insisted in 2004, "no one should feel sorry for me! I've paid my dues and I don't think there's anyone with more credibility than me. I am unique in the fashion world, and to be able to do what I like and have a viable company makes me very privileged. I offer a choice to people in an age of conformity."[175]

The year 2006 would also be a turning point when her collections crossed into the overtly political. Her designs had always been about subversion and provoking the establishment, but the message was often one people had to search for within the intellectualism and historical references. The Autumn/Winter 2005 collection, Propaganda, was a cry against consumerism, and from now on, she would use her clothing like slogan tees, to deliver the messages that were important to her; namely, fighting for liberty, anti-consumerism and the environment.

The roots of the Propaganda collection were an essay by Aldous Huxley, *Propaganda in a Democratic Society*, which described three pillars of suffering: nationalist idolatry, non-stop distraction and organized lying. Models wore headbands with "Branded", and as an update of her slogan T-shirts from the '70s, they now had Huxley quotations, and slogans like "Fuck everybody but US". The show was also an opportunity to campaign for the freedom of Leonard Peltier, the Native American activist who was found guilty of murder in 1977, and for whom Nelson Mandela and Amnesty had called to be released.

The punk ethos was never too far away from Vivienne, yet she was also becoming firmly part of the establishment. In 2005, as part of the queen's New Year's Honours List, Vivienne was made a Dame of the British Empire. She was presented with

RIGHT A model in Agent Provocateur "Fair Trial My Arse" knickers on the catwalk for Vivienne's Autumn/Winter 2008 show at London Fashion Week.

OPPOSITE The I Am Expensiv collection for Spring/Summer 2007 was, according to Vivienne, a message about the privilege of Western society and its exploitation around the world.

the award by the then Prince Charles at Buckingham Palace, and while she had once criticized it, she was now a defender of the Crown. She believed it was a mistake "to think that because some traditional things should be done away with, you have to throw them all out".[176]

Her next collection, Active Resistance, for Spring/Summer 2006, was a follow-up to Propaganda as she used slogan messaging, and with her models dressed as warriors, to protest against the British government's proposed anti-terrorist legislation. This idea also tapped into Innocent, for Autumn/Winter 2006, which was a tribute to witches burned at the stake, and a reference to Peltier's imprisonment. There were hooded gowns, draped togas

LEFT Model wearing Vivienne Westwood Wake Up Cave Girl! collection, Autumn/ Winter 2007, during Paris Fashion Week.

in hardier fabrics, and pagan symbols, and one model even had a bag over her head, like the prisoners held in Guantanamo Bay.

Just as she had taken aim at Disney with her slogan T-shirts, she cast a childlike eye over the collection. She based her lead character on an amalgamation of Disney princesses, while also specifying it had been designed for a fantasy American heiress looking for a wealthy husband. She used children's scrawls in primary colours for the backdrop and on fabric, which, of course, carried a political message that tied with the show's title as a protest against wealth accumulation.

Her Autumn/Winter 2007 show, Wake Up Cave Girl!, was a tribute to women in history, with folded fabric manipulated to enhance the body. She considered it to be like carving a statue, but with cloth, and she and Andreas nicknamed the technique "Wilma", after the Flintstones character, as if the simplicity was from the Stone Age. The finale of the collection, the "Cloud" wedding gown, with its voluminous, ivory silk duchess satin and the corset with its angular bust, would become one of the most famous of all when it was adopted by Carrie Bradshaw in *Sex and the City*.

OPPOSITE The famed wedding dress from *Sex and The City* the movie was the finale of the Wake Up Cave Girl! collection, shown at Paris Fashion Week in February 2007.

THE CORSET

"You can build something grand, if you start with a corset," Vivienne once explained, "because it holds up so much fabric. You can have a train that goes halfway down the catwalk, with a corset."[177]

When Vivienne brought her "Stature of Liberty" corset to the runway for the Harris Tweed collection in 1987, she not only reintroduced an item of clothing that hadn't been fashionable since the '50s, but she transformed the feminine silhouette. The corset had, for decades, been considered one of the trappings of patriarchy in its constraint of women, but Vivienne sought to redefine it as empowering and to elevate it from underwear to outerwear.

She tapped into the extravagance of the eighteenth century, when corsets constructed from multi-panels and whalebones were designed to cinch the waist, and to lift and push together the breasts. Vivienne took the original design but offered shape and flexibility with stretch panels to provide postural support. She further enhanced the rococo aesthetics by designing them in sensual satin, lace and brocade, and printed with Boucher art for the Portrait collection. She also added a practical zip detail so that women could put them on themselves. The corset would become an integral component of both her Gold Label and Red Label collections, and the corset structure within her gowns instilled confidence in women of all ages and body shapes. As she embraced the erotic power of an historical garment, she also ensured they were liberating, so that her revival of the corset became one of the most important fashion innovations of the last decades of the twentieth century.

CLOCKWISE FROM TOP Denise Lewis and Susie Bick hit the headlines when they kissed during the Portrait show; a corset from the Always on Camera collection, Autumn/Winter 1992; Bella Hadid in a Vivienne Westwood orb logo corset, 2018.

OPPOSITE *Shepherd and Shepherdesses* by François Boucher, 1760.

9

POP CULTURE MAVEN

OPPOSITE Tracy Emin with Vivienne and her husband Andreas Kronthaler at the Turner Prize awards ceremony, at Tate Britain in November 1999. Emin was nominated for her installation *My Bed*.

When photos were released of Sarah Jessica Parker as Carrie Bradshaw in a voluminous wedding gown, hoisting up the billowing folds of cream silk satin to stop her from tripping, it led to two major questions – who designed the dress and was she really getting married? The scene was from the much-anticipated *Sex and the City* movie, which was released in 2008, bringing new levels of attention to Vivienne Westwood and her bridal gown.

It was only after shooting had begun that Vivienne became aware that her gown would be featured in the new film, when Sarah Jessica Parker expressed her adoration of it. Other designers had submitted their creations, featured in a dress-up montage, and to Vivienne's surprise, the actress and producer chose hers as the main event. The wedding dress, with its strapless bodice as pointed as angel wings, was from the Gold Label Autumn/Winter 2007 Wake Up Cave Girl! collection, and took inspiration from the diamond cutting technique. Costume designer Patricia Field added a further eccentricity with a turquoise-plumed bird as headwear. "I wasn't sure about the green feather," said Vivienne, "but that dress is a divine archetype; it lives, as it were, in Plato's wedding heaven! And I wrote the note in the film, I did do that, pretending it was the real thing."[178]

"THAT DRESS IS A DIVINE ARCHETYPE; IT LIVES, AS IT WERE, IN PLATO'S WEDDING HEAVEN!"

Carrie, in the movie, receives a handwritten note from Vivienne, "Dear Carrie, I saw your photo from the *Vogue* shoot. This dress belongs to you! Love, Vivienne Westwood." If Carrie was thankful to Vivienne, then the designer owed a debt of gratitude to the film. She may have walked out of the premiere after ten minutes because she was unimpressed

ABOVE Emma Thompson in a chocolate Vivienne Westwood corseted gown at the world premiere of *Nanny McPhee and the Big Bang* in London, March 2010.

OPPOSITE Sarah Jessica Parker on location in New York City during the filming of *Sex and The City*, 12 October 2007.

by the fashion on display, but it helped to protect her brand from the recession. Sales rose by nearly a fifth in 2008 thanks to the publicity, as it led to a whole new following of style-conscious young women who considered Carrie Bradshaw a style goddess, and to an increased demand from celebrities who also wanted some of the magic.

From 2008 onwards, Vivienne's designs became a staple of red-carpet events, for film premieres to major events like the Academy Awards and the Grammys. In 2010, Emma Thompson wore a chocolate strapless Westwood design to the London premiere of *Nanny McPhee and the Big Bang* when she was accompanied by her husband, daughter and a pig. And in 2011, Helen Mirren chose a similar brown satin dress at the Academy Awards. These actresses were appreciative of the structure and comfort that Vivienne's corseted gowns brought to them, and a decade later, a new generation of hot young things, from Bella Hadid to Zendaya and Dua Lipa were all choosing Vivienne Westwood as an edgy statement to showcase their insider fashion credentials.

From her earliest forays as a designer on the King's Road, when she and Malcolm McLaren were the anarchic duo who catered to dedicated style tribes like the Teddy boys and rockers, Vivienne was surrounded by celebrity. Musicians, models and those with a hunger for fame were drawn to each incarnation. The Sex Pistols swore on television in her concepts; Chrissie Hynde worked the till and flashed her buttocks in black suspenders and rubber; Alice Cooper rocked in the risqué T-shirts; and Siouxsie Sioux and Adam Ant were regulars as they honed their goth and new romantic stage looks. The punks of the Bromley Contingent and the New Romantic Blitz kids possessed a natural showmanship that would make them stars – members of Bananarama and Spandau Ballet, Boy George, DJ Jeremy Healy and John Galliano would all be drawn to Vivienne and her Pirate and Buffalo collections because they were so tuned in with what was happening on a street level.

Vivienne's designs were a cross-pollination of fashion, music and art, and just as Malcolm ensured that the Sex Pistols and Bow Wow Wow were dressed in pieces from the shop, musicians would continue to be drawn to her as she entered a new phase in the 1990s. In 1993, Duran Duran commissioned Vivienne to

ABOVE Duran Duran in 1981, with John Taylor (second from right) in the Pirate rope print shirt.

design clothes for *The Wedding Album* tour and for the music videos from that album, 'Ordinary World', 'Come Undone' and 'Too Much Information'. Duran Duran, with their new wave synth sound, had emerged from the New Romantic scene in 1980 as they showcased the DIY punk and glam rock aesthetic with pieces bought from Worlds End and PX boutiques. The band's John Taylor even wore the rope-patterned shirt from the Pirate collection in one publicity photo. Their music comeback in the early '90s coincided with Vivienne's rise in fortunes and reputation. Looking back on some of their style moments, Nick Rhodes told *Vogue*, "We've always loved her, she's been amazing since the punk days and all those incredible pieces they made at Seditionaries. I think the mid '90s was a golden era for her."[179]

When Barbra Streisand asked Vivienne to design the costumes for her London concert at Wembley in 1994, her first

"WE'VE ALWAYS LOVED HER, SHE'S BEEN AMAZING SINCE THE PUNK DAYS ... I THINK THE MID '90S WAS A GOLDEN ERA FOR HER."

Nick Rhodes

performance in Britain for over 20 years, the news caused a stir. The British press particularly enjoyed the contrast between the singer, more known for her conventional sounds and safe, muted wardrobe, and the eccentric designer whose catwalk shows were so often a provocation of phallic symbolism and nudity.

In a piece in the *Daily Mirror*, Barbra was described as "brave" for wearing "Britain's most outrageous designer". Barbra, the article stated, preferred sedate designs by Donna Karan and Giorgio Armani. In comparison, Vivienne's flesh bodysuits, jewelled codpieces and fur bikinis were treated as laughably outrageous and her "repertoire included bondage trousers, rib-crunching bustiers and ten-inch high sequined platform shoes".[180]

As another article in the *Daily Mirror* sniggered: "One shudders to think of the whacky gimmick she will design for Barbra. We can only keep our fingers crossed that the 51-year-old singer draws the line at the no-knicker look which Viv sported at a party to celebrate her OBE last year."[181]

According to Jane Mulvagh's biography of Vivienne, Barbra had been impressed by photographs of Vivienne's empire-line blouses and ballgowns in an editorial in *The New York Times Magazine*, and she contacted the designer's office to request something similar be custom-made. She selected muted tones – black, white and marron glacé – for gowns and suits that would be worn to her London show, for an appearance before Bill Clinton at the presidential gala and for a special show in Los Angeles. However, Vivienne Westwood's team failed to meet the deadline for alterations and fittings, shipping the gowns to the States when it was too late to fix them; a situation which Mulvagh said highlighted "the chaotic and unprofessional workings of Vivienne's studio".

One commission that went smoothly was for Kate Winslet, who was one of the first stars to wear Vivienne Westwood on the Oscars red carpet. She chose a candy pink corseted gown at the 1996 Academy Awards when she was nominated for her role in *Sense and Sensibility*. While she didn't go home with the Oscar, she found out shortly after that she was cast in *Titanic*, so maybe the oomph of Vivienne's corseted gown helped a future A-list star make a strong impression.

The following year, in 1997, Helena Bonham Carter chose to wear a pink corset gown for the premiere of *The Wings of the*

"VIVIENNE STARTED OFF A PUNK AND ENDED AS A DAME, WITHOUT COMPROMISING AN INCH."

Helena Bonham Carter

OPPOSITE Helena Bonham Carter at the gala screening of *The King's Speech* at Odeon Leicester Square, London, October 2010.

BELOW Kate Winslet in pink Vivienne Westwood, for the 68th Annual Academy Awards, 1996.

Dove. Bonham Carter, often making her own headlines for her eccentric dress, became a longtime fan and friend of Vivienne's, regularly choosing her for the red carpet, such as when she wore mismatched shoes at the 2011 Golden Globes, and collecting her CBE in 2012 at Buckingham Palace in a Lochcarron of Scotland suit. Following Vivienne's death, she appeared on *The Graham Norton Show* sofa wearing seven pieces of Vivienne Westwood, including a "penis" print skirt which she had previously worn on the show. "Vivienne believed in buy less, so I thought I'd wear exactly the same thing," she said. She also praised the support of the corset "which means you can eat anything. I've been eating cake, but it doesn't really matter because it shoves that and makes these things happen," she added, pointing to her cleavage.

For her Autumn/Winter 2000 collection in Paris, entitled Winter, Bianca Jagger and Mel B, aka Scary Spice from the Spice Girls, were on the front row, and walking on the catwalk, in front of a quotation from Shakespeare's *Love's Labour's Lost*, was Tracey Emin. The artist's erotic pieces fused with Vivienne's sexually charged designs and the two had struck up a friendship when they met on a *Vogue* shoot in 1999. Tracey was running late due to trying to finish her work for the Turner Prize. "The traffic was horrific, and by the time I got there, I was in a really foul mood. Someone from *Vogue* asked if there was anything they could get me, and I said I needed some cigarettes. Then someone walked over and handed me a Gitane – and when I looked up, it was Vivienne Westwood. She said, 'If you think you've got a problem, I've been here for hours!'"[182]

The two kept in touch, and Tracey Emin would become a model for the brand, as well as choosing Vivienne for her own wardrobe. She later claimed that the art world accused her of being a sell-out for their collaboration, but she insisted there were no contracts: "I did it because I liked Vivienne and what she stood for."[183]

She followed the same sustainable ethos, of keeping hold of the same clothes and continuing to wear them: "My oldest Westwood ballgown is 22 years old, and I wear it all the time still," Emin said in 2024. "We've put seams in it, we've altered it, we've made it smaller, we've made it bigger. On every big occasion that I have, I wear the same dress. The other thing about Vivienne is that being an older woman, you can still wear

TAMARA DREWE
GLAMOUR
GIRL

LEFT Vivienne with Tracey Emin at the Chaos Point Gala Dinner, where the designer presented her Gold Label collection in aid of NSPCC, 2008.

Westwood and look cool, because Westwood clothes are so comfortable. Everybody thinks that Westwood is all about being wild and crazy, but there's a whole mix in there."[184]

While the common belief in the 1990s was that Vivienne Westwood was only for the most daring, this assumption overlooked the comfort and support brought by her corsetry. Nigella Lawson in 2004 made clear that she relied on a select few Vivienne Westwood favourites for the safety she felt in the corseted gowns, as if they melded to her body. While she had initially thought, "I was far too bosomy and would look like I was applying for a part in some sort of porn film", she told British *Vogue*: "I know I won't bulge or slip or need to start tugging at hemlines ... In a way I feel her clothes are the anti-fashion, which suits me perfectly."

There was a particular dress that Nigella would return to again and again – a made-to-measure "Cocotte" dress in black, which

RIGHT Nigella Lawson in her treasured Cocotte dress at the launch party of the New Saatchi Gallery in London, April 2003.

was corseted and off-the-shoulder. She was first seen wearing it in March 2003 for her future husband Charles Saatchi's opening of his new gallery on London's Southbank. A month later she wore it on *The Tonight Show with Jay Leno* in the United States. She also wore the same dress to promote her new cookbook, *Feast*, in 2004.

"Fashion gurus might warn the Domestic Goddess that it's a risk to look the same on every occasion, but clearly she knows what she likes," wrote one newspaper. In response, a spokesperson for the designer said: "She loves that black dress ... and it loves her. She has a really good figure. That dress gives you a great bust, pulls you in at the waist and gives a lot of leg exposure. Everything a woman wants."[185]

While Vivienne had been commissioned to create costumes for underground movies in the '70s, her designs were selected for a mainstream Hollywood film for the first time in 1995.

"EVERY TIME I GO TO LONDON, I HAVE TO BUY THREE SUITS. HER CLOTHES FIT ME REALLY WELL. THEY'RE MODERN, CLASSIC AND EVERYTHING THAT I LOVE."

Gwen Stefani

Director Mike Figgis chose Vivienne Westwood corsets for Elisabeth Shue in *Leaving Las Vegas*. While she was playing a sex worker, he thought Vivienne's designs weren't "whorish", but instead conveyed an empowerment. To prepare for the role Figgis asked Elisabeth Shue to wear the corset and mini on Sunset Boulevard, and her appearance almost stopped traffic. When the film received Oscar nominations, including for Best Director, Vivienne gave Figgis a set of penis and vulva cufflinks to wear with his suits, and as a thank you, he made sure to name-check her in publicity for the film.

By the 2000s, Vivienne's status was now as a pop culture reference point whose vintage fashions were being sought out by fashionistas, as sparked by Kate Moss in the Pirate boots. In November 2000, Vivienne was convinced by her publicity team in LA to make more celebrity connections, and so she held a show in the palm tree-studded gardens of the Sunset Marquis in West Hollywood. Her PRs invited Amanda de Cadenet, hot young actresses of the day Shannon Elizabeth and Emilie de Ravin, and even Roseanne Barr. "It's been explained to me that these days, it's not so much that you want Christy Turlington on the cover of your magazine. You want – well, I don't know who you want," Vivienne told the *Los Angeles Times*.[186]

It was Vivienne's designs that helped guide the fantastical, high-fashion aesthetics for Gwen Stefani's first solo single and album in 2003. The singer told the *Associated Press* in 2005 that the only "real designer that I give all my money to is Vivienne Westwood. Every time I go to London, I have to buy three suits. Her clothes fit me really well. They're modern, classic and everything that I love."[187]

In the promo for her first solo single, 'What You Waiting for?', she took on Alice in Wonderland vibes while wearing custom-made Vivienne Westwood, including a tartan corset and pale-blue miniskirt. She also namechecked Vivienne in tracks from her album *Love. Angel. Music. Baby.* In 'Rich Girl' she thinks of all she could buy, including everything in a Vivienne Westwood store, while rocking a Galliano gown.

Gwen Stefani's promotion of Vivienne Westwood in 2004 also tied in with her appreciation of Tokyo's Harajuku subcultures, in which fashion-conscious teens and 20-somethings created a unique and expressive amalgamation of designer brands, kitsch

ABOVE Vivienne with Dita Von Teese (l) and Gwen Stefani (r) at the Vivienne Westwood Diamond Party, during Paris Fashion Week, March 2005.

and colourful labels, and Japanese tradition. Vivienne was lauded in the country, and the Lolita street style had a Vivienne aura with the girlish Alice in Wonderland bell skirts and DIY attitude.

Then, with her exhibition at the Victoria and Albert Museum in 2004, there was a further appreciation of the punk designer. Kate Moss had led the way with her vintage finds, such as the Pirate boots, which were relaunched after she was snapped in them. At the opening night gala, the supermodel raved that "I've loved her since I was 14. I used to make special trips to London to buy her clothes."[188]

A few years before the film *Sex and the City*, another bridal gown had made headlines, this time for a real-life bride, when burlesque star Dita Von Teese chose an unconventional and dramatic taffeta purple gown for her wedding to Marilyn Manson in 2005. Dita revealed on the *No Gorge* podcast in December 2023 that it was red and blue silk woven together, and that "I flew to London to meet Vivienne and I remember I got sent into her office ... and she had sketched out this dress that was red and it had orange and red flames, and it was ripped out everywhere, and I had to tell her I didn't like the idea, and that I wanted something more classical ... she dismissed me, and put it all on her husband, who oversaw my dress, and it's one of the most beautiful things to come out of the couture."

The Costume Institute's 2013 exhibition "Punk: Chaos to Culture" sparked a new trend for punk on the catwalk for

autumn 2013, and with that year's Met Gala theme devoted to the punk of the exhibition, the celebrity radar was further refocused on Vivienne. Kim Kardashian wore stark white Westwood to the Met Gala in 2017, and in 2018 Thandiwe Newton wore a custom-made gown printed with images of the Black actors who had appeared in the *Star Wars* franchise to the 2018 Cannes Film Festival. Hailey Bieber and Miley Cyrus both took after Dita Von Teese in choosing Westwood for their weddings, with Cyrus in ivory silk from the bridal collection in 2018, and Bieber in a white corseted minidress for the rehearsal dinner in 2019.

OPPOSITE Actress Thandiwe Newton wearing a custom-made gown printed with Black characters from Star Wars, for the screening of *Solo: A Star Wars Story* at the 71st annual Cannes Film Festival, May 2018.

Members of the royal family were also choosing Vivienne, a Dame of the British Empire, for their occasion dressing. She may have crashed the Silver Jubilee in 1977 with her scathing satirical T-shirts that rivalled the official souvenir merchandise, but she had also imbued her collections with tradition. The Queen's Diamond Jubilee in 2012 inspired a Red Carpet Capsule Collection of draped corset gowns that were universally flattering.

Princess Eugenie wore a blue two-piece outfit to the wedding of Prince William and Catherine Middleton, and the night before the ceremony a long, black corseted Vivienne Westwood gown. The designer, however, was more critical of Catherine's style. "I would have loved to have dressed Kate Middleton," she said. "But I have to wait until she kind of catches up a bit somewhere with style."

Camilla, Duchess of Cornwall, was also a fan, having worn a blue taffeta Vivienne Westwood gown to the Royal Variety Performance in 2008, and like her husband, was a supporter of the designer's climate initiatives. Vivienne even dedicated her Autumn/Winter 2015 menswear show in Milan to Prince Charles for his environmental work, and she came out at the end of the show wearing a dress emblazoned with a photographic print of his face. It seemed fitting that for the new king's coronation in May 2023, pop star Katy Perry would ask the Westwood design house, just four months after Vivienne's death, to design her outfit. The creation was a lilac jacket and matching skirt made from leatherette sourced from the archives, and accessorized with a three-row pearl bas-relief choker and granny frame pearl handbag.

By the 2020s, modern It girls with an eye for cutting-edge vintage had fully embraced the treasures of past Vivienne Westwood collections. In September 2019, Bella Hadid, who also walked the Westwood runway as a muse, teamed a pair of khaki pants with a corset printed with the eighteenth-century Boucher painting of *Hercules and Omphale* kissing, from the Autumn/Winter 1993 Anglomania collection. There was a vintage corset with orb logo worn in New York in winter 2018, and when celebrating her first solo American *Vogue* cover, she was snapped in a knitted floral top from On Liberty in Autumn/Winter 1994.

In 2015, for her first ever Academy Awards, an 18-year-old Zendaya, along with her long-term stylist Law Roach, selected a custom-made Vivienne Westwood bridal gown. Zendaya also chose vintage Westwood when promoting her 2024 film *Challengers*, by wearing a pinstripe waistcoat and matching feather bustle miniskirt from the Spring/Summer 1994 Café Society collection.

Opting for vintage Vivienne Westwood, whether it was a slogan T-shirt, the three-tier pearl and orb necklace or a vintage corset, was a savvy means of demonstrating insightful fashion knowledge in scouring for vintage finds, as well as impeccable, and edgy tastes. It wasn't just the girls bringing back vintage Westwood. Pharrell Williams revived the Buffalo hat from the Autumn/Winter 1983 collection, when he wore it to the 2014 Grammy Awards. Vivienne's showmanship ensured her designs were a perfect fit for red carpet events and for performances. Dua Lipa wore a white silk top and skirt to the 2020 Grammy Awards and then a Union Jack trench coat at the 2021 Brit Awards.

Of all her muses, the one who was completely tuned in to the same political and environment causes was Pamela Anderson. They first met when Pamela was a guest at the Spring/Summer 2009 show at London Fashion Week. As part of the Man collection Vivienne had included a cotton "Leonard Peltier is innocent" T-shirt, which was printed with an image of Peltier and a group of children behind him. She and Anderson both bonded over their interest in campaigning for the freedom of the Native American activist, and as their close friendship developed, Pamela became the new face of the label. She walked the Autumn/Winter 2009 catwalk at Paris Fashion Week, wrapped in a lilac tutu lifted like angel wings, and in October 2013, Pamela asked Vivienne to dress her for the *Ellen* show in something suitably punk rock. For the next decade she would also be in the front row of her shows, and they both bonded over their causes; the championing of PETA, and their support of Julian Assange, with Pamela helping arrange for Vivienne to visit him in the Ecuadorian embassy, where he had sought sanctuary from extradition to the United States.

When Carrie Bradshaw wore the "cream puff" of a bridal gown, it led to speculation that it "could bring back the trend of poufy 80s-era wedding dresses".[189] Fifteen years later, in the *Sex and the City* television revival *And Just Like That*, Carrie brought the wedding gown out of her closet when she was looking for a last-minute outfit to wear to the Met Gala. This time she wore

ABOVE Pharrell Williams wearing the Buffalo hat for the announcement of the Academy Award nominations, February 2014.

OPPOSITE Bella Hadid (r) wearing a corset from the Always on Camera collection, printed with François Boucher's *Hercules and Omphale*. With Alana Hadid, New York, September 2019.

LEFT Charli XCX with a breast-printed harness bag, at the Vivienne Westwood Red Label show during London Fashion Week, February 2016.

OPPOSITE Pamela Anderson and Vivienne Westwood at the end of the Autumn/Winter 2009 show during Paris Fashion Week, March 2009.

it with a teal cape, matching gloves and slingback heels, and coming full circle, it once again made headlines and promoted Vivienne as the pop culture designer. Although, she was often unsure exactly who these celebrities were. "I don't follow popular culture. I don't go to the cinema. When I go to social events, it can be quite embarrassing. If I see a really good-looking person, I think: 'Oh, that person must be famous!' But maybe they're not. I don't know the people. I do know Angelina Jolie because she's an activist. So I met her."[190]

Vivienne may have had an aversion to contemporary cinema and popular culture, but in 2021, the Disney movie *Cruella*, set in 1970s London, took her incarnation as the punk fashion designer as a basis for the outrageous lead character, Cruella de Vil. Jenny Beavan, the film's costume designer, remembered wandering down the King's Road in the early '70s. While she would buy pieces from Biba, she was "far too scared" to go into Let It Rock or SEX. "I sort of remember hovering on the step thinking I shouldn't. Because I was quite nervous and I think I was probably dressed in a rather sober and conventional way in those days ... But, you know, I remember just being intrigued."[191]

THE PEARL CHOKER

The three row pearl bas relief choker is one of Vivienne Westwood's most recent, and most popular, cult items. The choker is constructed with hand-strung and knotted glass-based Swarovski vegan pearls, which are then connected to the brass signature orb logo.

It was first shown in the Portrait collection, tying in with the decadence of the rococo-inspired gowns and the eighteenth-century portraits. Vivienne chose pearls for their complex symbolism: they have historically represented both purity and sexuality, and there is the famous story of Cleopatra dissolving hers in wine and then swallowing it as part of a bet.

Vivienne first showed pearls in the Harris Tweed collection as she parodied the twin-sets and pearls of *Tatler* society girls. It was in this collection that the Orb Saturn ring logo was first conceived, borrowing from the Harris Tweed authentication mark, while adding galactic rings. From then on, the orb logo appeared in every collection, whether it was printed on corsets, tops and scarves, or incorporated in jewellery.

The pearl choker gained a whole new cult following in the 2020s, when it was nick-named "the TikTok" necklace as influencers shared theirs on the app, unboxing them and layering them in different ways. Janelle Monáe wore one at Paris Fashion Week in 2020, while Dua Lipa's was a key part of her look at the BRIT Awards in London in 2021, and the necklace is a firm favourite of Bella Hadid, Rihanna and Kylie Jenner.

The relative accessibility of the piece, in comparison to vintage corsets and hard-to-find T-shirts, also encouraged its popularity. Proudly wearing one was a means of tapping into the revolutionary spirit of Vivienne Westwood, capturing the craze for Georgian style with the popularity of the TV series *Bridgerton*, and as an access point to owning the same cult item as fashion's new icons.

ABOVE Dua Lipa teaming the pearl choker with a Vivienne Westwood dress at The BRIT Awards, London, May 2021.

OPPOSITE Janelle Monáe in the front row at the Andreas Kronthaler for Vivienne Westwood show during Paris Fashion Week, February 2020.

CLIMATE
REVOLUTION

10

CLIMATE REVOLUTION

OPPOSITE After a dramatic launch at the Red Label show during London Fashion Week in September 2012, Vivienne devoted herself to the Climate Revolution campaign.

In March 2014, Vivienne appeared on stage at the Southbank Centre in a woven brown dress that sparkled under the light, her eyebrows pencilled in red, and her head now bald, except for wisps of white hair. The 72-year-old was fierce yet vulnerable as she spoke to the audience about the most important cause of her life – climate change.

With Spring/Summer 2008's 56, named after the number of days the British government proposed to detain people without trial under the new anti-terrorism legislation, her collections shifted from politics to focusing on saving the planet. For Chaos Point (Autumn/Winter 2008), Vivienne asked for primary school children to submit hand-painted designs of eco-warriors in the rainforest, using CHAOS and "Active Resistance" as slogans. These were then printed on jersey tops and toga dresses, faux sheepskin jackets and canvas bags as a statement of hope through the eyes of children.

"Punk was a heroic attempt at confronting the establishment. But ultimately it failed," Vivienne had said in 2000.[192] Now, out of all the campaigns Vivienne supported, climate change was the one she believed was the most critical. To help raise awareness she had taken a shaver to her trademark red hair and sheared her scalp, and first unveiled this new look during the March 2014 Paris Fashion Week. It was not only a call to wake up to climate change, but it was also a way of saying goodbye to the dyed locks, so she could be proud of her white hair, and of her age. She still blamed the older generation for the ills of the world, but she was also gratified

"PUNK WAS A HEROIC ATTEMPT AT CONFRONTING THE ESTABLISHMENT. BUT ULTIMATELY IT FAILED."

at having turned 70, with all the experience and wisdom that came with it. She had marked this new decade by posing gloriously naked for photographer Juergen Teller. Reclining on an antique gilt sofa, her soft red hair crowning her, she gloriously evoked Manet's *Olympia*.

At the Women of the World Festival at the Southbank Centre she was interviewed on stage by politician and human rights activist Baroness Shami Chakrabarti. She told her audience, "Buy less, choose well, make it last." She was also planning to practise what she preached with her own business. She was one of the most important figures in the fashion industry, but she vowed to limit fast fashion and encourage a more sustainable business model. Her company made a £5 million profit in 2012, up from the previous year, which was in part due to the opening of several new shops. But in 2014, she announced that she was dropping expansion plans in favour of making her fashion empire sustainable. "I have decided not to expand any more. In fact I want to do the opposite," she told the *Observer*. "I am now more interested in quality rather than quantity."

She was adamant that customers should be informed in their choices, and that they should prioritize buying clothing that would last. She was insistent that if people just bought a select few beautiful pieces, rather than cheap, disposable whims that were a blight on the world's vital resources and often went

ABOVE LEFT The +5° Autumn/Winter 2009 collection was inspired by painter Andrea Mantegna and the "Gaia" theory of James Lovelock.

ABOVE A "make do and mend" theme for the Do It Yourself Spring/Summer 2009 collection featured toga dresses from curtains and tablecloths.

"IT'S NOT GOOD TO JUST GO TO A SUPERMARKET AND COME BACK WITH BAGS AND BAGS OF CHEAP T-SHIRTS. ALL THIS CONSUMPTION IS NOT A REAL CHOICE."

straight to landfill, then climate change could be tackled. "In my view it is worse for someone to come out of a shop with an armful of new T-shirts made in a sweatshop, than it is for a rich lady to buy one beautiful dress," she again told the *Observer*.

There was a privilege to that statement, because most people didn't have the luxury or choice to be able to splurge on pieces that were priced at three, and even four, figures. During her Southbank Centre interview, she acknowledged that this ethos was difficult for those on limited budgets, given the financial crisis and the recession that followed, but she believed shopping at Primark was not the answer. "It is difficult for people. But I think it's not good to just go to a supermarket and come back with bags and bags of cheap t-shirts. All this consumption is not a real choice."

She had encouraged her audience at the Do It Yourself Spring/Summer 2009 collection to forge their own individual style. It returned to the punk ethos of safety pins, slogan T-shirts and badges, recycling and wartime "make do and mend", while also incorporating pagan draping, as if dresses had been constructed from tablecloths and curtains.

She was impassioned as she spoke of her major concern that the global population faced mass extinction, and that fashion was partly culpable. "Do I feel guilty about all the consumption that the fashion world promotes?" she asked. "Well, I can answer that by saying that I am now trying to make my own business more efficient and self-sustaining. This also means trying to make everybody who works in it happy, if I can."[193]

But she was also aware that she had two hundred people working for the company, which gave her responsibility to keep them in employment.[194] Instead, she would now use her platform as a world-famous designer to talk politics, and to do all she could to implement change and to protect the planet for the next generations to come. Vivienne had asked to be a guest on *The Jonathan Ross Show* in January 2010, so she could speak to a national audience about her concerns around climate change. She credited her passion to James Lovelock's 1972 work *Gaia*, a theory that the earth is a single organism working in synergy to self-regulate its heating and cooling systems. For Vivienne, it was a warning of catastrophe, one which it was estimated that the world's population would dwindle to one billion by the end of the century due to global heating.

It was in the 1970s that climate change first emerged as a threat, because scientists were uncovering evidence that increases in CO^2, along with waste heat, were having a cataclysmic impact on global temperatures. The term "global warming" was first used by US scientist Wallace Broecker, who included it in the title of his scientific paper in 1975. Frank Press, Science Advisor to President Jimmy Carter, sent a memorandum in 1977 warning that the greenhouse effect caused by atmospheric CO^2 would induce a global climate warming of 0.5 to 5 degrees centigrade, and that these effects, including large-scale crop failures, would become evident not long after the year 2000.

In February 1979, the same month that Sid Vicious was found dead, the World Climate Conference of the World Meteorological Organization declared that some global effects of carbon dioxide in the atmosphere warming earth would be evident by the end of the century. Environmental concerns were still not yet fully formed in the public's mind as punk began to fade, yet Vivienne's philosophy of promoting quality over quantity had been threaded into her early designs. This "make do and mend" attitude was part of her story, having been ingrained during her formative years spent under rationing.

As she designed her first catwalk shows in the '80s, her focus was on garments that were designed to last, and which used recycled materials. For Buffalo and Nostalgia of Mud she looked outside of Western culture by borrowing from the techniques of ethnic groups who often used recycled products for practical clothing designed to withstand the environment they lived in. It was a form of sustainability before the concept was widely understood. Both these collections referenced indigenous cultures of the American continent, and by the time she launched Climate Revolution, it was clear that indigenous people were the first to suffer from the effects of climate change.

The environment and animal rights became an increasing concern for Vivienne as interest in her label grew. She used fake fur for the first time in the Portrait collection, and in 1993 used photographic prints to highlight endangered animals in the Grand Hotel collection. At the time her rebellious nature made her suspicious of PETA, because she considered their anti-fur message a form of puritanism "that can't even allow you to think one way or another".[195] But in 1994, she spoke to *Women's*

RIGHT Vivienne at the Do It Yourself Spring/Summer 2009 show during Paris Fashion Week, September 2008.

Wear Daily about her concerns around consumerist culture and its effect on the environment. "We've been in a period of democratic envy, where people think it's bad to spend money on clothes," she said. "I think. I hope, people are starting to look at that differently now. We can't go on consuming the way we did. You can't go on exploiting the world in terms of quantity, so you have to do it in terms of quality."[196]

In 2014, she officially stopped using real fur in her collections, and now, as a full supporter of PETA, she took part in a campaign video, where she posed naked in the shower to raise awareness of how much water was consumed by the meat industry. "I am an eco-warrior, but I take long showers with a clean conscience because I'm vegetarian," she said in the video.

She first drafted a political and climate manifesto in 2007, in which she called for "active resistance to propaganda", as she fought against mass consumerism and aspects of modern culture that were integral to capitalism. Reading out this manifesto at the Wallace Collection, she was bringing it back to the place that had been so integral to the designs that had made her an international name.

Her anti-capitalist stance was considered radical, particularly as she called for a redistribution of wealth, yet it was the same message she had delivered in the '70s, when she used punk as a rallying cry for change. She didn't care about upsetting the powerful figures in the fashion industry, and with her usual forthrightness she told *The New York Times* in 2013: "America is an isolated territory, with all those editors who think they are so powerful. Mostly, I think they are rubbish. And I don't like fashion magazines either. Someone asked me the other day, if I really was a world controller, what is the first thing I would do. I would stop advertising."[197]

Her collection +5 for Autumn/Winter 2009 took its name from the rise in temperature that would have such a cataclysmic effect on the planet, and which, with its drapery inspired by ancient Greek art, was a tribute to the earth deity Gaia, and to Lovelock's theory.

"Gaia The Only One", for Spring/Summer 2011, was dedicated to the voluptuous female figure, and took the work of Matisse, Commedia dell'arte and ballet, and Peruvian girls "waiting to marry the sun", as its inspiration for the tutus, padded corsets, and folk costume. The Spring/Summer 2012 collection provided a "family tree" to her audience, outlining the connection to earth and science through the Gaia theory, and transforming the art lover into a "freedom fighter for a better world". The designs, combining Pirate with Chinese and Tuareg dress, featured enlarged corsets with sleeves and necklines that lifted from the body, as if they were armour for warriors.

Vivienne's new focus was revealed at the Paralympics in 2012 as she took to the stage as the warrior queen Boudica, unfurling a banner to launch Climate Revolution. The aim of the organization was to target environmental and political issues, and to work with other non-profits by speaking "with one voice". To coincide with it, in October 2012, she brought her Gold Label Climate Revolution collection (Spring/Summer 2013) to the catwalk in the British embassy in Paris. With a mishmash of inspirations, from the iridescence of beetles to the paintings of Velazquez, it featured slashed costumes, and the designs on a Chinese tea box. At its heart was a desire to reduce waste with her cutting techniques, such as the square T-shirts with just two panels of fabric sewn together.

From now on, she announced, she would be reforming her business as she focused on climate change, and would throw her considerable might behind anti-fracking, the Greenpeace Arctic Campaign and Cool Earth, a charity protecting rainforests with the help of the indigenous communities under threat from developers. She had made a considerable personal donation of £1 million to Cool Earth in 2009, and together with Andreas, she became their most ardent patron and supporter. She believed that the loss of rainforests was the greatest ecological threat, and that by halting their destruction it "could quite literally save the world". She also founded the Vivienne Foundation to partner with NGOs to help deliver the message that "tomorrow is too late", and that to save the world they needed to build on four pillars of change – to halt climate change, stop war, defend human rights, and protest against capitalism.

"SOMEONE ASKED ME THE OTHER DAY, IF I REALLY WAS A WORLD CONTROLLER, WHAT IS THE FIRST THING I WOULD DO. I WOULD STOP ADVERTISING."

In 2013, as part of her work with Cool Earth, she and Andreas spent a week living with a tribe in the Peruvian rainforest, as part of the Asháninka community project. They also lobbied the Peruvian government on their forestry programme to call for a protection of the country's rainforests. The costume worn by the Peruvian Asháninka tribe would be one of the inspirations for her Save the Rainforest collection for Autumn/Winter 2014. It was another homage to Charles Worth, taking as a starting point Franz Xaver Winterhalter's 1865 portrait of Empress Elizabeth of Austria, and combining it with the look of eco-warriors and anti-fracking slogans.

She designed a collection of T-shirts for Cool Earth, with proceeds going towards their work with local rainforest communities, and in 2018, she collaborated with Burberry in support of the organization to launch a special collection that recreated

ABOVE The Metropolitan Museum's Costume Institute's "Punk – Chaos to Couture" opened to the press on 6 May 2013, New York. The exhibition examinesd punk's impact on high street fashion, from the birth of the movement in the 1970s to today.

OPPOSITE Slogan T-shirt as part of the Red Label Spring/Summer 2013 collection, when the Climate Revolution was launched.

some of her classic pieces from Anglomania in the signature Burberry check.

Her campaigning was also attracting celebrity voices. Lady Gaga was photographed wearing a Spring/Summer 2013 Climate Revolution T-shirt within 24 hours of its catwalk debut. "I get credibility from doing the fashion, which helps me as a propagandist, gives me a voice. People will listen to you. That's one reason I think it's important to carry on."[198]

As part of her support of Greenpeace's efforts to Save the Arctic, she worked with photographer Andy Gotts to take portraits of celebrities including Jerry Hall, George Clooney, Chris Martin, Paloma Faith and Monty Python's Terry Jones and Terry Gilliam, which were then displayed at London's Waterloo Underground station in 2013. "Public opinion is very responsive to celebrity," she said. "The first thing I tend to do is ask them for a small amount of money, something that means nothing to them. Then they feel involved, rather than as if they are just doing me a favour."[199]

Her campaigning for action on climate change and for Liberty often meshed together. At the Met Gala in May 2013, with its Chaos to Couture punk theme, she pinned to her pink silk coat a photograph of whistleblower Chelsea Manning with TRUTH written underneath. She and husband Andreas were accompanied by the model Lily Cole, who was wearing a custom-made Amazonian wild rubber dress.

Peace
+5°
Yes

ABOVE Vivienne with the frown painted on her face, and Climate Revolution across her chest, as she launches the campaign during London Fashion Week in September 2012.

OPPOSITE Calling for Active Resistance in the 56 collection for Spring/Summer 2008, which protested the British government's planned new counter-terrorism legislation which could imprison people without trial for 56 days.

On the red carpet, every question about what she was wearing was a chance to highlight the photo that was displayed prominently on her clothes. "I'm here to support Manning. That's the most important thing I want to say," she said pointedly. Lily Cole later reflected in an article in *Vogue* in 2023 that she and Vivienne bonded over "the language of visual activism". They collaborated together on a number of occasions, with the Amazonian wild rubber dress at the Met Gala and a recycled-plastic dress at the Oscars, and after performing a pagan dance for the Spring/Summer 2014 Red Label show in London, she handed out cards to raise awareness of climate refugees. "Over the years, we discussed many topics, yet I don't recall ever discussing fashion," Cole said.[200]

"IF PEOPLE AREN'T AWARE, HOW ARE WE GOING TO SAVE THE WORLD FROM CORRUPTION AND CLIMATE CHANGE?"

"Everything is Connected" was the slogan for Climate Revolution and it formed the title of her Spring/Summer 2014 collection, where she hammered home the message that everything we do can make

ABOVE Vivienne riding on a tank heading towards the then Prime Minister David Cameron's home in Oxfordshire on 11 September 2015, to protest against fracking.

a difference. By this time, she was actively involved in protesting against fracking, a process of extracting oil and gas from deep underground, by using the attention-grabbing stunts of the punk era to make her points. She led a protest in Balcombe, Sussex by riding a bus into a field and meeting locals in the pub to warn them of how fracking would impact on house prices. In February 2015, angry at Prime Minister David Cameron's support of it, she sat on top of a tank and defiantly drove it to the front door of his home in the village of Chadlington, Oxfordshire.

In December 2014, she and her son Joe, accompanied by Father Christmas in a gas mask, attempted to deliver a parcel of asbestos to Downing Street as a special Christmas present for David Cameron. But her irresponsible plan was stopped by police officers who didn't allow this potentially deadly package through. Instead, she was able to pass on an open letter from Talk Fracking, which was signed by 150 high-profile supporters, including Stella McCartney and Helena Bonham Carter. She also included a file of research into the dangers of the process, which linked the chemicals used in fracking to birth defects, cancers and skin diseases.[201]

The idea of protest via asbestos had been cemented when Malcolm McLaren died from cancer in 2010. He was just 64 years old, and his partner Young Kim was convinced that his diagnosis

ABOVE Vivienne with Peter Gabriel and Emma Thompson at The People's March for Climate in London on 21 September 2014, to demand urgent action on climate change.

of mesothelioma, a form of lung cancer, was caused by exposure to asbestos at the SEX shop. He had demolished the ceiling to make it look like a bomb had hit it, and this is believed to have disturbed the asbestos insulation.

If there was one project that at first seemed at odds with her ethos, it was her collaboration with Virgin Atlantic in 2014, when Richard Branson, an old friend from the punk days, asked her to design new staff uniforms. She created sustainable 1940s-inspired tailored suits, partly constructed from a polyester made from used plastic bottles, developed by a new Closed Loop Recycling technology. "The hardest thing to cut down is flying," she acknowledged. "Suppose I want sustainable cotton. I'm not going to get it from England. I get it from Peru. I try not to travel so much, but shipping stuff is madness. So, if I were Richard Branson, I wouldn't be stopping my airline. At the moment, he's trying to develop oil fuel algae and I don't know what else."[202]

Unisex – Time to Act for Autumn/Winter 2015 brought together her menswear and womenswear collections for the first time since 1996. Playing with gender, it wasn't just trousers for women; she wanted men in dresses, and manipulated the size and structure of shoulder pads and Grecian silhouettes. Every new collection and catwalk show was also now a place of protest. Just before showing her Spring/Summer 2016 collection

“ALL MY MOTIVATION HAS BEEN BECAUSE I HAVE BEEN SO UPSET ABOUT WHAT CAN HAPPEN TO PEOPLE IN THE WORLD.”

at London Fashion Week, she published a letter warning of mass extinction due to climate change.

She led a procession of demonstrators, dressed in leggings and shorts, with bright crowns and red lipstick, from outside the venue and onto the catwalk as they held placards reading “Climate Revolution” and “Austerity is a Crime”. The show itself, entitled Mirror the World, was set in Venice, the sinking city, to highlight the dangers of climate change. She used renaissance art and Byzantine treasures to highlight the messages of austerity, and the paganism of the carnival to create surrealist masks. This would be the final show for Vivienne Westwood Gold Label. From now on Andreas would take the reins under a new name, Andreas Kronthaler for Vivienne Westwood.

Given her championing of sourcing local, she moved her collections back to London Fashion Week, with her Autumn/Winter 2017 collection being the first in London since the ’80s. The Autumn/Winter 2018 collection railed against everything from global warming to Brexit and free speech. “All my motivation has been because I have been so upset about what can happen to people in the world,” she said. “That’s had something to do with my fashion clothes.”

In an interview with *The New York Times* in 2020, she said that since her days of punk, she had been an activist, fighting for human rights and against capitalism. “On social media, I’m dressing up every week for my Friday speeches, using my fashion to get people involved in politics. If people aren’t aware, how are we going to save the world from corruption and climate change?”[203]

As a promotional part of her campaigning, she designed a pack of playing cards which each featured a strategy to save the world, and she was absolutely convinced that her ideas were the key.

As much as it was about performance, it was absolutely clear to Vivienne what she needed to do to combat the climate crisis. For COP26, held in Glasgow in 2021, she released a recording of her speech at Shakespeare’s Globe in London as she called for action against climate change and a land-free economy. “Reduce, reuse, recycle” was her message, and one that connected with a new cohort of switched-on young people – Generation Z, who were similarly concerned about climate change and the threat to the environment.

OPPOSITE Vivienne with her son, Joseph Corré, and models and activists, to protest against fracking during London Fashion Week, February 2018.

BELOW Vivienne wearing a paper crown, while attending The People’s March for Climate, Justice and Jobs in November 2015.

FRACKING
Won't
FRACKING
CLIMATE
CHAOS
INE

THE POLITICAL ACTIVIST

From her early statement T-shirts, bondage trousers and anarchy "A" logos, Vivienne's work was driven by a desire for change and to challenge the status quo. She was unafraid to confront the issues she cared about, using her skills in publicity and happenings to raise awareness through stunts that would capture the imagination of both the press and the public. This included the unforgettable sight of the septuagenarian on top of a tank being driven to Prime Minister David Cameron's home as a form of protest.

Some of Vivienne's causes and campaigns have included Amnesty International, Reprieve, which supports prisoners on death row and those who have been wrongfully imprisoned, and the UK civil liberties organization Liberty, for which her "I am not a terrorist" T-shirts and babygrows were bestsellers.

Her political campaigning included fights on behalf of Julian Assange, Chelsea Manning and Leonard Peltier. At the opening of the "Chaos to Couture" exhibition in 2013, she harked back to her punk origins by pinning a "Free Chelsea Manning" image on her dress, and in 2020, to protest against Julian Assange's extradition, she dressed as a yellow canary in a cage outside Downing Street.

ABOVE Vivienne collaborated with human rights group Liberty in September 2005, to launch a T-shirt and Baby-gro to protest the British government's new anti-terror law.

When she posed as Margaret Thatcher for the cover of the April 1989 edition of *Tatler*, it wasn't out of admiration, rather it was a parody, given how out of step they were politically. In the 1990s, she was particularly concerned about the effect that cuts were having on cultural institutions, such as the Victoria and Albert Museum and the Natural History Museum. Staff were being made redundant and she worried about how that would impact on caring for the collections, and the education and learning opportunities for visitors.

Yet she also used her catwalk to provoke and spark conversation. There were the moments that pushed at societal hang-ups, with Sara Stockbridge taking to the catwalk when she was heavily pregnant, and having two models on the Portrait collection catwalk kiss one another to mimic the Daphnis and Chloe painting that was printed on their corsets. Previously, Sara Stockbridge and Susie Bick, dressed as harlequins for Voyage to Cythera in 1989, shared a kiss, and that moment, in a collection rife with provocative fig leaves, caused a stir in the papers.

She showed her support for Scottish independence at her Red Label Autumn/Winter 2014 London Fashion Week show

ABOVE Vivienne with Andreas, showing her support for Prince Charles in the finale of her menswear show in Milan Menswear Fashion Week, January 2015.

when models paraded in "Yes" badges, as she believed the Scottish independence referendum campaign "could be the turning point towards a better world". She later told reporters: "I like Scotland because somehow I think they are better than we are. They are more democratic."

With her impassioned support of the environment and her deep concerns about climate change, she threw her name behind PETA, the Environmental Justice Foundation, Friends of the Earth and Cool Earth as her catwalk collections after 2012 became a form of protest. First launched at the Paralympics, Climate Revolution became her primary cause, as she dressed her models as eco-warriors and protesters with placards. Her Autumn/Winter 2015 menswear collection was a tribute to Prince Charles's environmental campaigns, and the models sported bruised faces making it hard to look away.

11

FINAL YEARS

OPPOSITE Vivienne during London Fashion Week in February 2019, as she walks the runway for her Autumn/Winter 2019 show.

Vivienne had struggled financially throughout the '80s and early '90s, despite her high-end ready-to-wear innovations – the slogan tee, the corsets with printed images, the tube skirt, the mini-crini – being profitable to others. She reinvented herself from queen of punk to a student of history and art who absorbed intellectual concepts and translated them into clothing that was steeped in the past. At a time when Calvin Klein and Donna Karan were establishing a minimalistic aesthetic of plain white tees and silk slips, Vivienne's 1990s designs were a confection of rococo and exaggerated femininity. Her menswear collections were imbued with an appealing swashbuckling spirit, with asymmetric suits, embroidered shirts, buffalo hats and kilts, and she promoted a gender defiance with her male models in dresses. Ultimately, she believed that cutting was her major contribution to fashion, and the key to her success, with this deconstruction inspiring other designers like Rei Kawakubo of Comme des Garçons and Yohji Yamamoto. "The principles came from ethnic clothes, and older patterns. Like that very first T-shirt I started with that used the whole width of the cloth. All in rectangles. Nothing wasted. Very 'utility'. Very 'historical,'" she said.[204]

"WE NEED TO GET BACK TO HAVING FEWER THINGS, AND TREASURING WHAT WE HAVE. THAT'S WHY I DEFEND HIGH FASHION."

Now in her seventies, the grande dame was still an eccentric who wore mismatched clothing, and who continued to cycle around London with her much younger husband. They worked together in the Battersea studio, sketching and draping and cutting new designs, as theirs was very much a collaboration of ideas. Her policy was to downsize the

ABOVE The Andreas Kronthaler for Vivienne Westwood Autumn/Winter 2019 show, at London Fashion Week, February 2019.

OPPOSITE Vivienne's granddaughter, Cora Corré, walks the runway for the first show after her death Autumn/Winter 2023, at Hotel de la Marine, Paris, 4 March 2023.

business, and by 2020 her collections were 50 per cent smaller than they had been three years before, and were sold at a higher price point. Whereas, she had previously kept costs down, now she believed in couture over high street, and that the key was buying less, and buying clothes to last. She considered cotton a luxury due to the environmental footprint, and so insisted that the T-shirts be sold for £100 or more. "We need to get back to having fewer things, and treasuring what we have. That's why I defend high fashion," she said. "But of course, we need a fair distribution of wealth."[205]

Vivienne's message around punk was conflicted. While she often described it as a failure, at other times she declared her pride in being part of it. "I think it really did implant a message that was already there," she told *The New York Times* in 2013. "The hippies told it to me, but punk made it something cool for people to stand up for, which is that we do not believe government, that we are against government."[206]

But in 2016, she and her son Joseph Corré controversially set fire to £5 million worth of punk memorabilia on a barge on the Thames, as a protest against its commercialism. "It's all gone. I'm not interested. What I say about punk is that I considered it a marketing opportunity, more or less, and that's why I got out of it. It was kids having a great time, jumping and spitting, but for what? Sell more razor blades, sell more safety pins? I don't know."[207]

"IF YOU LOVE SOMETHING WEAR IT ALL THE TIME, DON'T JUST SUCK IT ALL UP AND CONSUME. FIND THINGS THAT SUIT YOU. THAT'S HOW YOU LOOK EXTRAORDINARY."

Vivienne also railed against the industry she was an integral part of: "I don't follow fashion. I really don't. I've never been interested in it." As much as she rejected it, she had become an icon for a younger demographic who had been brought up with the climate crisis and the instability of terrorism as a backdrop to their childhoods. Generation Z were switched on to political and environmental causes, and they admired her for her activism. Now that the fashion industry was under the spotlight for its impact on the planet's resources, buying into Vivienne's brand was a way of aligning with the environmental cause. "Choose well and make it last," she advised readers of *Miss Vogue*. "If you love something wear it all the time, don't just suck it all up and consume. Find things that suit you. That's how you look extraordinary."[208]

It didn't hurt that her key pieces were being shared on TikTok along with snaps of the latest fashion It girls wearing the bas-relief pearl choker, the corsets and slogan T-shirts.

In 2016, after passing control of the Gold Label line to Andreas, she became less involved in the design process. Her interviews, including one in *GQ* in 2021, had become a pulpit where she could regale journalists with her politics, while the fashion was of much less interest to her. Her climate change manifesto was a 12-page e-book furnished with collages, drawings and texts and she wrote regularly on climate and social justice issues on her website No Man's Land. It was named after the "No Man's Land" economy, where if no one owns land, it can't be exploited.[209]

In July 2020, she performed another publicity-grabbing stunt on behalf of Julian Assange. Wearing a canary yellow trouser suit, she suspended herself in a 10-foot (3-metre) birdcage outside the Old Bailey in London, where the WikiLeaks founder was expected to appear for an extradition hearing that September. She was dressed in yellow, she explained, because canaries were used by miners to detect poisonous gas. "If the canary died they all got out. Julian Assange is in a cage and he needs to get out. Don't extradite to America." Ultimately, the extradition was delayed (and cancelled in 2024), and in 2022 she designed the outfits for both Assange and fiancée Stella for their wedding.

When the pandemic hit, she and Andreas spent lockdown focusing on "Activism, working on my strategy to save the world, cooking". She was also single-minded in spreading her climate

OPPOSITE Vivienne held an exhibition at the Serpentine Gallery during London Fashion Week in February 2020. It showcased her latest collection while protesting on behalf of Julian Assange.

I can do
easy 4 me
born
a duty 2 do
my best
K
UE PUNK
Assange.”
K

OPPOSITE Bella Hadid turned heads in a sheer lace wedding dress, complete with knife belt, for the Autumn/Winter 2020 Andreas Kronthaler for Vivienne Westwood collection during Paris Fashion Week, February 2020.

message through her Friday speeches shared on her Climate Revolution website and on social media, where she dressed up every time in something from the archive. "The pandemic is sending us back to our personal resources," she said. "For me, art is timeless; it stops the clock. It really is an imitation of reality. And great art is as relevant in the present as it was when it was created."[210]

Despite suffering from ill health, Vivienne was determined that her work would be continued after she was gone. She gave her support to the Stop Oil activists who threw soup and paint at important artworks, as much as she believed in the importance of galleries. "Young people are desperate. They're doing something," she wrote on her blog in 2022.

On 29 December 2022, it was announced that 81-year-old Vivienne had passed away in her Clapham home, surrounded by family. She had been working right up until the last moments, still designing, still creating art and writing. She was buried in the Derbyshire hills of her childhood, which she had once described as the "most beautiful place in the world".

After a private family funeral, her memorial was held at Southwark Cathedral in February 2023, on the eve of London Fashion Week, with guests including Kate Moss, Victoria Beckham, Anna Wintour and Chrissie Hynde dressed in tribute to the designer. There were corsets, devil-horn tiaras and ropes of pearls, swathes of tartan, biker jackets, platform shoes and large pink top hats.[211]

"Vivienne started off a punk and ended as a dame, without compromising an inch," Helena Bonham Carter said as she

"FOR ME, ART IS TIMELESS; IT STOPS THE CLOCK. IT REALLY IS AN IMITATION OF REALITY. AND GREAT ART IS AS RELEVANT IN THE PRESENT AS IT WAS WHEN IT WAS CREATED."

"I AM A TEACHER, A TAOIST, AN ACTIVIST, AN ARTIST AND WELL ... A DESIGNER."

delivered her eulogy. She described how she had bought her first Vivienne Westwood piece, a white shirt from the Pirate collection, at the age of 15, and that her wardrobe had been stuffed with Westwood, with seven "Cocotte" dresses.

She recalled a reporter having asked why she wore only Westwood on the red carpet. "Because she's a genius," she replied. Bonham Carter described her as "a true feminist and lover of women" who devoted her life to activism.[212] She added, "Thank you for the cutting, the draping that makes your clothes so dynamic and alive, so much so that I wouldn't be surprised to wake in the night and find them dancing in my closet, alive."[213]

When Vivienne was asked by her granddaughter Cora how she would define herself, she would reply, "I am a teacher, a taoist, an activist, an artist and well ... a designer." As Cora addressed the audience at the memorial, she implored them to honour Vivienne by sharing "your stage, shed light on the issues and speak up for the people that don't have a voice, and let Vivienne's fight continue through you. We need more people like Vivienne in the world."[214]

For his first collection after his wife's death (Autumn/Winter 2023), Andreas ensured it was a cathartic means of celebrating her life by creating sustainable designs that were a patchwork of deadstock and recycled fabric. It was also infused with the classic Vivienne Westwood designs of high platforms, mid-length crinolines, tartan skirts over printed tights, the buckled pirate boots, and a T-shirt featuring her image.[215]

Vivienne's was a story against the odds. She was a working -class northern English woman who had finally achieved the success and acknowledgement she deserved when she was in her fifties. She headed up her own label, ensuring it remained independent from the major fashion conglomerates. Despite the continued growth and popularity, she chose to pare it back to reinforce her anti-consumerist principles and her all-consuming desire to save the planet and the environment from destruction.

OPPOSITE Vivenne Westwood portrait, 2009.

INDEX

Page numbers in *italics* refer to illustrations

ENDNOTES

1 Jewelers Circular Keystone, "Vivienne Westwood debuts 'Hardcore': 'High Priestess of Punk' goes precious", Hedda Schupak, June 2005
2 *WWD*, "Westwood's Way", Samantha Conti and Ellen Burney, 1 April 2004
3 *Newsweek International*, "Rebellion by Design", Tara Pepper, 2 May 2004
4 *WWD*, "Viva Vivienne!", Amy Spindler, 18 November 1992
5 *Newsweek International*, "April 08 1941", Tara Pepper, 3 May 2004
6 *WWD*, "Westwood's Way", Samantha Conti and Ellen Burney, 1 April 1 2004
7 The *Independent*, "Meet the grande dame of Glossop", 19 October 1999
8 The *Telegraph*, "Family Detective", Nick Barratt, 24 February 2007
9 Fury, Alexander, *Vivienne Westwood Catwalk: The Complete Collections* (Thames & Hudson, 2021)
10 The *Telegraph*, "Family Detective", Nick Barratt, 24 February 2007
11 *The Times*, "Time and place: Dame Vivienne Westwood", Angela Wintle, 19 April 2015
12 Mulvagh, Jane, *Vivienne Westwood: An Unfashionable Life* (Harper Collins, 2003)
13 Westwood, Vivienne, and Ian Kelly, *Vivienne Westwood* (Picador, 2014)
14 ibid
15 ibid
16 *The Times*, "Time and place: Dame Vivienne Westwood", Angela Wintle, 19 April 2015
17 Westwood, Vivienne, and Ian Kelly, *Vivienne Westwood* (Picador, 2014)
18 *Desert Island Discs*, Vivienne Westwood, 28 June 1992
19 Mulvagh, Jane, *Vivienne Westwood: An Unfashionable Life* (Harper Collins, 2003)
20 The *Independent*, "Meet the grande dame of Glossop", 19 October 1999
21 *The Times*, "Time and place: Dame Vivienne Westwood", Angela Wintle, 19 April 2015
22 Westwood, Vivienne, and Ian Kelly, *Vivienne Westwood* (Picador, 2014)
23 Mulvagh, Jane, *Vivienne Westwood: An Unfashionable Life* (Harper Collins, 2003)
24 Westwood, Vivienne, and Ian Kelly, *Vivienne Westwood* (Picador, 2014)
25 ibid
26 ibid
27 The *Guardian*, "Westwood ho!", Alix Sharkey, 8 April 2001
28 ibid
29 *Desert Island Discs*, Vivienne Westwood, 28 June 1992
30 *Harper's Bazaar*, "Vivienne Westwood: 'I am unique in the fashion world'", Rebecca Lowthorpe, March 2004
31 ibid
32 *Desert Island Discs*, Vivienne Westwood, 28 June 1992
33 Westwood, Vivienne, and Ian Kelly, *Vivienne Westwood* (Picador, 2014)
34 ibid
35 Mulvagh, Jane, *Vivienne Westwood: An Unfashionable Life* (Harper Collins, 2003)
36 Westwood, Vivienne, and Ian Kelly, *Vivienne Westwood* (Picador, 2014)
37 ibid
38 *The New York Times*, "Vivienne Westwood: At 71, Still Not Done Provoking", Eric Wilson, 5 March 2013
39 The *Guardian*, "How playing cards can save the planet and the pure bliss of falling in love", Jess Cartner-Morley, 15 February 2020
40 Mulvagh, Jane, *Vivienne Westwood: An Unfashionable Life* (Harper Collins, 2003)
41 The *Guardian*, Westwood ho!, Alix Sharkey, 8 April 2001
42 Westwood, Vivienne, and Ian Kelly, *Vivienne Westwood* (Picador, 2014)
43 Mulvagh, Jane, *Vivienne Westwood: An Unfashionable Life* (Harper Collins, 2003)
44 *The Sunday Times Magazine*, Valerie Wade, 14 May 1972
45 *Evening Standard*, "Jeremy Debonnaire, better-known as Pinky the Greaser", Maureen Cleave, 9 June 1972
46 Fury, Alexander, *Vivienne Westwood Catwalk* (Thames & Hudson, 2021)
47 Westwood, Vivienne, and Ian Kelly, *Vivienne Westwood* (Picador, 2014)
48 Mulvagh, Jane, *Vivienne Westwood: An Unfashionable Life* (Harper Collins, 2003)
49 Fury, Alexander, *Vivienne Westwood Catwalk* (Thames & Hudson, 2021)
50 Mulvagh, Jane, *Vivienne Westwood: An Unfashionable Life* (Harper Collins, 2003)
51 *WWD*, "Viva Vivienne!", Amy Spindler, 18 November 1992
52 The *Guardian*, "Punktuation", Angela Neustatter, 23 September 1977
53 The *Guardian*, "They had the T-shirt off his back", Nicholas de Jongh, 2 August 1975
54 Mulvagh, Jane, *Vivienne Westwood: An Unfashionable Life* (Harper Collins, 2003)
55 ibid
56 *Harper's Bazaar*, "Vivienne Westwood: 'I am unique in the fashion world'", Rebecca Lowthorpe, March 2004
57 Mulvagh, Jane, *Vivienne Westwood: An Unfashionable Life* (Harper Collins, 2003)
58 Westwood, Vivienne, and Ian Kelly, *Vivienne Westwood* (Picador, 2014)
59 Mulvagh, Jane, *Vivienne Westwood: An Unfashionable Life* (Harper Collins, 2003)
60 *Harper's Bazaar*, "Vivienne Westwood: 'I am unique in the fashion world'", Rebecca Lowthorpe, March 2004
61 Westwood, Vivienne, and Ian Kelly, *Vivienne Westwood* (Picador, 2014)
62 The *Washington Post*, "London Punk Rockers Outdo the Hippies", Nina S. Hyde, 4 May 1977
63 ibid
64 Westwood, Vivienne, and Ian Kelly, *Vivienne Westwood* (Picador, 2014)
65 Mulvagh, Jane, *Vivienne Westwood: An Unfashionable Life* (Harper Collins, 2003)
66 ibid
67 Westwood, Vivienne, and Ian Kelly, *Vivienne Westwood* (Picador, 2014)
68 The *Guardian*, "Punktuation", Angela Neustatter, 23 September 1977
69 ibid
70 The *Independent*, "Vivienne Westwood: Disgracefully yours, the Queen Mother of Fashion", 2 June 2002
71 *The Sunday Telegraph*, "Design on the Times", Kathy Phillips, 11 March 1990
72 *WWD*, "Forever Viv", Janet Ozzard, 13 September 1994
73 Mulvagh, Jane, *Vivienne Westwood: An Unfashionable Life* (Harper Collins, 2003)
74 ibid
75 *Evening Standard*, Fashion, Liz Smith, 10 November 1980
76 *Vogue*, "Why the Swagger of Vivienne Westwood's 1981 Pirate Collection Resonates 40 Years On", Laird Borrelli-Persson, 17 May 2021
77 Westwood, Vivienne, and Ian Kelly, *Vivienne Westwood* (Picador, 2014)
78 Mulvagh, Jane, *Vivienne Westwood: An Unfashionable Life* (Harper Collins, 2003)

79 *Evening Standard*, Fashion, Liz Smith, 10 November 1980
80 The *Observer*, "The wilder shores of fashion", Ann Boyd, 25 January 1981
81 *Vogue*, "Why the Swagger of Vivienne Westwood's 1981 Pirate Collection Resonates 40 Years On", Laird Borrelli-Persson, 17 May 2021
82 *The New York Times Magazine*, "Being and Nothingness and Kate Moss", Holly Brubach, 21 May 1995
83 *WWD*, "Westwood's Way", Samantha Conti and Ellen Burney, 1 April 2004
84 Mulvagh, Jane, *Vivienne Westwood: An Unfashionable Life* (Harper Collins, 2003)
85 Westwood, Vivienne, and Ian Kelly, *Vivienne Westwood* (Picador, 2014)
86 Mulvagh, Jane, *Vivienne Westwood: An Unfashionable Life* (Harper Collins, 2003)
87 ibid
88 ibid
89 *AnOther* magazine, "Vivienne Westwood's radically chic Nostalgia of Mud", Yvonne Gold, 15 March 2016
90 Westwood, Vivienne, and Ian Kelly, *Vivienne Westwood* (Picador, 2014)
91 *Desert Island Discs*, Vivienne Westwood, 28 June 1992
92 Westwood, Vivienne, and Ian Kelly, *Vivienne Westwood* (Picador, 2014)
93 Mulvagh, Jane, *Vivienne Westwood: An Unfashionable Life* (Harper Collins, 2003)
94 *Harper's Bazaar*, "Getting the Boot", Shane Watson, 1 March 2001
95 ibid
96 *WWD*, "Viva Vivienne!", Amy Spindler, 18 November 1992
97 *WWD*, "Westwood sings the praises of the crinoline", Susan Alai, 27 January 1986
98 ibid
99 *Evening Standard*, "The spring of the sweet young flirt", Jane Procter, 21 October 1986
100 *Desert Island Discs*, Vivienne Westwood, 28 June 1992
101 *WWD*, "Vivienne Westwood revives Worlds End", 8 July 1986
102 Westwood, Vivienne, and Ian Kelly, *Vivienne Westwood* (Picador, 2014)
103 Mulvagh, Jane, *Vivienne Westwood: An Unfashionable Life* (Harper Collins, 2003)
104 Westwood, Vivienne, and Ian Kelly, *Vivienne Westwood* (Picador, 2014)
105 *WWD*, "Westwood sings the praises of the crinoline", Susan Alai, 27 January 1986
106 Westwood, Vivienne, and Ian Kelly, *Vivienne Westwood* (Picador, 2014)
107 The *Observer*, "London Calling", Sarajane Hoare, 22 March 1987
108 *The Scotsman*, "Dame Vivienne Westwood: How the 'visionary' designer put the punk into Scotland's textile industry", Alison Campsie, 20 December 2022
109 *WWD*, "Westwood sings the praises of the crinoline", Susan Alai, 27 January 1986
110 Mulvagh, Jane, *Vivienne Westwood: An Unfashionable Life* (Harper Collins, 2003)
111 *Evening Standard*, "Suspendered disbelief", 27 July 1988
112 Westwood, Vivienne, and Ian Kelly, *Vivienne Westwood* (Picador, 2014)
113 *The Sunday Times*, "Fashion: Tightening their belts – London designers are no longer the wild bunch of fashion", Charlotte Du Cann, 20 March 1988
114 *The Sunday Times*, "No leading ladies – liberation at last", Rebecca Tyrrel, 16 October 1988
115 *Toronto Star*, "Westwood show aims to shock", Rebecca Bragg, 23 March 1989
116 *WWD*, "Westwood shows camp and vamp", 17 October 1989
117 ibid
118 Mulvagh, Jane, *Vivienne Westwood: An Unfashionable Life* (Harper Collins, 2003)
119 The *Guardian*, "Westwood ho!", Alix Sharkey, 8 April 2001
120 Mulvagh, Jane, *Vivienne Westwood: An Unfashionable Life* (Harper Collins, 2003)
121 *WWD*, "Paris: What's coming", William Middleton, 8 October 1996
122 The *Independent on Sunday*, "The Lynn Barber Interview: Vivienne Westwood", 18 February 1990
123 The *Guardian*, "Westwood ho!", Alix Sharkey, 8 April 2001
124 The *Sunday Telegraph*, "Design on the Times", Kathy Phillips, 11 March 1990
125 The *Guardian*, "Westwood ho!", Nilgin Yusuf, 25 March 1991
126 The *Sunday Telegraph*, "Design on the Times", Kathy Phillips, 11 March 1990
127 *WWD*, "The gang of four hits Tokyo", 12 December 1990
128 Fury, Alexander, *Vivienne Westwood Catwalk* (Thames & Hudson, 2021)
129 The *Guardian*, "Westwood ho!", Nilgin Yusuf, 25 March 1991
130 Fury, Alexander, *Vivienne Westwood Catwalk* (Thames & Hudson, 2021)
131 Mulvagh, Jane, *Vivienne Westwood: An Unfashionable Life* (Harper Collins, 2003)
132 *WWD*, "London shows: wacky is out and safe is in", 15 October 1990
133 The *Guardian*, "Westwood ho!", Nilgin Yusuf, 25 March 1991
134 ibid
135 ibid
136 ibid
137 *GQ*, "Andreas Kronthaler: 'When I came to Britain, I was young and very, very sexy'", Matthew Whitehouse, 7 December 2018
138 *Vogue*, "Vivienne Westwood Is Remembered In London", Luke Leitch, 17 February 2023
139 The *Guardian*, "Westwood ho!", Alix Sharkey, 8 April 2001
140 *W* magazine, "Forgotten runway, Vivienne Westwood Fall '92 channeled Marlene Dietrich at her chicest", Kristen Bateman, 5 September 2022
141 *WWD*, "Westwood tops low-key London Shows", 16 March 1992
142 *WWD*, "Westwood takes Fifth Ave", Janet Ozzard and Sharon Edelson, 16 September 1994
143 *WWD*, "Viva Vivienne!", Amy Spindler, 18 November 1992
144 *Harper's Bazaar*, "Vivienne Westwood: 'I am unique in the fashion world'", Rebecca Lowthorpe, March 2004
145 *Daily Mirror*, "High Fashion – Viv gives Naomi a big hand", Karen Kay, 21 October 1993
146 *WWD*, "Forever Viv", Janet Ozzard, 13 September 1994
147 *WWD*, "Westwood takes Fifth Ave", Janet Ozzard and Sharon Edelson, 16 September 1994
148 ibid
149 *WWD*, "Forever Viv", Janet Ozzard, 13 September 1994
150 *Daily Mirror*, 3 November 1993
151 ibid
152 *Daily Mirror*, "Catwalk to Catalogue", Ollie Picton-Jones, 26 October 1994
153 The *Independent*, "Westwood makes up for lost time with hourglass look", Tamsin Blanchard, 20 March 1995
154 *WWD*, "Forever Viv", Janet Ozzard, 13 September 1994
155 *WWD*, "As buyers hit Paris, designers prepare a feast of fashion", William Middleton, 12 March 1996
156 *WWD*, "Paris: What's coming", William Middleton, 8 October 1996
157 *WWD*, "Paris", 17 March 1997
158 *WWD*, "Westwood beckons with boudoir", James Fallon, 26 June 1998
159 ibid
160 The *Independent*, "Westwood spins a ship-wrecked theme", Melanie Rickey, 18 October 1997
161 *WWD*, "Vivienne Westwood has just discovered the 20th century", 16 March 1998
162 *Los Angeles Times*, "Still an original", Booth Moore, 24 November 2000
163 *WWD*, "Westwood licenses Anglomania", James Fallon and Luisa

Zargani, 25 May 2001
164 The *Independent*, "Vivienne Westwood: Disgracefully yours, the Queen Mother of Fashion", 2 June 2002
165 *Los Angeles Times*, "Still an original", Booth Moore, 24 November 2000
166 *Harper's Bazaar*, "Vivienne Westwood: 'I am unique in the fashion world'", Rebecca Lowthorpe, March 2004
167 *Los Angeles Times*, "Still an original", Booth Moore, 24 November 2000
168 *Harper's Bazaar*, "Vivienne Westwood: 'I am unique in the fashion world'", Rebecca Lowthorpe, March 2004
169 The *Guardian*, "Westwood ho!", Alix Sharkey, 8 April 2001
170 *Harper's Bazaar*, "Westwood, Ho!", James Scully, August 2001
171 *The Sunday Times*, Planet Fashion, Claudia Croft, 1 April 2001
172 The *Daily Telegraph*, "When only Westwood would do", Clare Coulson, 1 April 2004
173 Jewelers Circular Keystone, "Vivienne Westwood debuts 'Hardcore': 'High Priestess of Punk' goes precious", Hedda Schupak, June 2005
174 *WWD*, "Vivienne Westwood's $600 safety pins", 28 February 2005
175 *Harper's Bazaar*, "Vivienne Westwood: 'I am unique in the fashion world'", Rebecca Lowthorpe, March 2004
176 *The Sunday Times*, "Anarchy in the UK – more like God save the Queen", 1 January 2006
177 The *Guardian*, "How playing cards can save the planet and the pure bliss of falling in love", Jess Cartner-Morley, 15 February 2020
178 Westwood, Vivienne, and Ian Kelly, *Vivienne Westwood* (Picador, 2014)
179 *Vogue*, "Eighties icons Duran Duran on their best style moments ever", Alex Kessler, 22 October 2021
180 *Daily Mirror*, "Can she do anything for Barbra?", Karen Kay, 30 March 1994
181 *Daily Mirror*, Fiona McIntosh, 30 March 1994
182 *Vogue*, "As Vivienne Westwood's Archive Goes To Auction, Tracey Emin Models Her Late Friend's Maverick Fashion", Tracey Emin, 11 June 2024
183 ibid
184 ibid
185 *Daily Mirror*, "That your favourite dressing, Nigella?", Deborah Sherwood, 12 December 2004
186 *Los Angeles Times*, "Still an original", Booth Moore, 24 November 2000
187 *Associated Press*, "Gwen Stefani pulls double duty as both singer and fashion designer to rave reviews", Samantha Critchell, 1 September 2005
188 *WWD*, "Westwood's Way", Samantha Conti and Ellen Burney, 1 April 2004
189 *Los Angeles Times*, "Style Notebook", Booth Moore, 25 May 2008
190 *New Statesman*, "Vivienne Westwood: 'I don't think about posterity at all'", Mark Lawson, 25 July 2014
191 *Los Angeles Times*, "How Vivienne Westwood's 'radical' work inspired 'Cruella's' Oscar-winning looks, Mark Olsen and Matt Brennan, 30 December 2022
192 *Los Angeles Times*, "Still an original", Booth Moore, 24 November 2000
193 The *Guardian*, "Fashion designer teams up with George Clooney, Chris Martin and Paloma Faith to back Arctic campaign", Vanessa Thorpe, 8 February 2014
194 *Harper's Bazaar*, "The Only Punk Left", Kathryn Flett, 5 February 2013
195 *WWD*, "Viva Vivienne!", Amy Spindler, 18 November 1992
196 *WWD*, "Forever Viv", Janet Ozzard, 13 September 1994
197 *The New York Times*, "Vivienne Westwood: At 71, Still Not Done Provoking", Eric Wilson, 5 March 2013
198 *Harper's Bazaar*, "The Only Punk Left", Kathryn Flett, 5 February 2013
199 *Vogue*, "As Vivienne Westwood's Archive Goes To Auction, Tracey Emin Models Her Late Friend's Maverick Fashion", Tracey Emin, 11 June 2024
200 *Vogue*, "'She Called Truths Out to Us All': Lily Cole Remembers Her Friend Vivienne Westwood", Lily Cole, 16 February 2023
201 *Evening Standard*, "Vivienne Westwood and son attempt to deliver asbestos to David Cameron in protest against fracking", 18 December 2014
202 *New Statesman*, "Vivienne Westwood: 'I don't think about posterity at all'", Mark Lawson, 25 July 2014
203 *The New York Times*, "Turning points: The World According to Vivienne Westwood", Vivienne Westwood, 5 December 2020
204 Westwood, Vivienne, and Ian Kelly, *Vivienne Westwood* (Picador, 2014)
205 The *Guardian*, "How playing cards can save the planet and the pure bliss of falling in love", Jess Cartner-Morley, 15 February 2020
206 *The New York Times*, "Vivienne Westwood: At 71, Still Not Done Provoking", Eric Wilson, 5 March 2013
207 *New Statesman*, "Vivienne Westwood: 'I don't think about posterity at all'", Mark Lawson, 25 July 2014
208 *Vogue*, "Vivienne Westwood Is The Modern It Girl's Label Of Choice", Naomi Pike, 5 November 2019
209 *GQ*, "Dame Vivienne Westwood: 'Boris Johnson has never had an altruistic thought. He's completely destructive'", Teo van den Broeke, 3 September 2021
210 *The New York Times*, "Turning points: The World According to Vivienne Westwood", Vivienne Westwood, 5 December 2020
211 *The New York Times*, "Farewell to Vivienne Westwood, Fashion's Rebel With a Cause", Elizabeth Paton, 17 February 2023
212 ibid
213 *Vogue*, "Vivienne Westwood Is Remembered In London", Luke Leitch, 17 February 2023
214 British *Vogue*, "A Year On From Vivienne Westwood's Memorial, Her Granddaughter Cora Corré Shares Her Personal Tribute", Cora Corré, 16 February 2024
215 The *Guardian*, "Just weeks after her death, Vivienne Westwood's rule-defying spirit lives on in Paris show", Morwenna Ferrier, 4 March 2023

PICTURE CREDITS

The publishers would like to thank the following contributors for supplying images for this book, with special thanks to Platon.

Alamy Stock Photo: adrian lourie 23; Associated Press 10–11; Chronicle 62; Goddard Archive 2 89; Homer Sykes 50 (bottom); Imagedoc 108–9; Independent 158–9; jeremy sutton-hibbert 8 (left); PA Images 127; Peter Horree 166; Roger Hutchings 150; Trinity Mirror / Mirrorpix 78; WENN Rights Ltd 80, 203.

Bridgeman Images: Everett Collection 182; Image Jamie Reid, copyright Sex Pistols Residuals 52 (left).

Getty Images: Alexis DUCLOS / Contributor 136, 144, 149 (left); Antonio de Moraes Barros Filho / Contributor 205; Astrid Stawiarz / Contributor 114; Bernard Weil / Contributor 95; Bertrand Rindoff Petroff / Contributor 119; CARL COURT / Stringer 198–9; Catherine McGann / Contributor 56; Dave Benett / Contributor 97, 112, 113, 126, 129, 168, 209, 211; Dave M. Benett / Contributor 176, 202; Dave Hogan / Contributor 75; David Corio / Contributor 70; David Montgomery / Contributor 60; Denis O'Regan / Contributor 67; DEUTSCH Jean-Claude / Contributor 7; Dimitrios Kambouris / Staff 196; Erica Echenberg / Contributor 59 (left); Evening Standard / Stringer 38; Fairchild Archive / Contributor 54; Ferdaus Shamim / Contributor 171; Florilegius / Contributor 99; Foc Kan / Contributor 109 (right); Francois Durand / Stringer 185; Gareth Cattermole / Staff 197; George Pimentel / Contributor 180; Getty Images / Staff 152; Gotham / Contributor 167 (bottom left), 183; Guy Marineau / Contributor 123, 125 (top), 132, 133; Ian Dickson / Contributor 48; Ian Gavan / Stringer 106, 124; Indianapolis Museum of Art at Newfields / Contributor 77; James Devaney / Contributor 170; Janette Beckman / Contributor 172; JMEnternational / Contributor 186; JOEL ROBINE / Contributor 145; John Stoddart/ Popperfoto / Contributor 88, 92; John van Hasselt - Corbis / Contributor 167 (top); Jon Furniss / Contributor 175; Justin Goff / Contributor 177; LEON NEAL / Staff 200; LUCAS BARIOULET / Contributor 212; Michael Ochs Archives / Stringer 49; Michael Putland / Contributor 79; Michael Webb / Stringer 34–5; Michel Dufour / Contributor 179; Michelle Leung / Contributor 164; Mike Marsland / Contributor 8–9, 188; Mirrorpix / Contributor 12, 19 (right), 24, 28, 31, 32, 36, 39, 46, 47, 50 (top), 63, 100, 120, 122, 137 (top); Nathan Shanahan / Stringer 17; Neil Mockford / Contributor 81, 153; PATRICK KOVARIK / Contributor 130; Penske Media / Contributor 40, 53, 98, 143 (left), 146, 147; Pierre VAUTHEY / Contributor 140; Pool ARNAL/GARCIA / Contributor 117, 131, 149 (right); Pool ARNAL/PAT / Contributor 128; Pool ARNAL/PICOT / Contributor 143 (right); Pool SIMON/STEVENS / Contributor 154–5, 157; Popperfoto / Contributor 18–19, 21; Ricky Vigil M / Contributor 184; Science & Society Picture Library / Contributor 134; Stephane Cardinale - Corbis / Contributor 155 (right); Steve Granitz / Contributor 174; Steve Wood/ Popperfoto / Contributor 139; Victor VIRGILE / Contributor 105, 121, 158 (left), 206, 208; Virginia Turbett / Contributor 65; WWD / Contributor 68, 71, 84, 85, 86, 107, 118, 187.

© Photography by Platon: 2, 215.

Shutterstock: ANL 74, 90; Cavan Pawson/ANL 163; Clive Dixon 59 (right), 93; Clive Dix 103 (right); Clive Limpkin/ANL 91; David Dagley 44, 45; Elisa Leonelli 6; Glenn Copus 104; Guignebourg-Nebinger-Taamallah/ABACA 165; Guindani Stefano 160; ITV 51; Ken Towner/ANL 148; Khayat-Nebinger-Orban-Taamallah/ABACA 199 (right); Lucas Dolega/EPA 190 (left); Michael Fresco/ANL 110; Mike Hollist/ANL 138; Nebinger-Orban-Taamallah/ABACA 190 (right); Neville Marriner/ANL 111, 141, 167 (bottom right); Nils Jorgensen 43, 52 (right), 125 (bottom), 137 (bottom); Norman Lomax 22; Olivier Hoslet/EPA 16; Orban-Taamallah-Zabulon/ ABACA 4–5, 162; Paul Massey 115; Phil Rees 64; Philip Hollis 14–15; Richard Young 72, 73, 159 (right); SGP 193; Shutterstock 156, 204.

TopFoto: PA 103 (left); PA Images / alamy 29; PA Photos 201; Photoshot / Picture by Laurie Lewis / Retna Pictures 82; Photoshot / Bandphoto / uppa.co.uk 102.

Published in 2025
by Gemini Gift Books
Part of Gemini Books Group

Based in Woodbridge and London

Marine House, Tide Mill Way,
Woodbridge, Suffolk IP12 1AP
United Kingdom

www.geminibooks.com

Designed by Goldust Design
Text by Caroline Young

ISBN 978-1-78675-172-0

A CIP catalogue record for this book is available from the British Library.

Manufacturer's EU Representative: Eurolink Compliance Limited, 25 Herbert Place, Dublin, D02 AY86, Republic of Ireland. admin@eurolink-europe.ie

Printed in China

10 9 8 7 6 5 4 3 2 1